SIZE ZERO

SIZE ZERO

MY LIFE AS A DISAPPEARING MODEL

VICTOIRE DAUXERRE

with Valérie Péronnet

translated from the French by Andy Bliss

WILLIAM
COLLINS

William Collins
An imprint of HarperCollins*Publishers*
1 London Bridge Street
London SE1 9GF

WilliamCollinsBooks.com

First published in Great Britain by William Collins in 2017

1

A catalogue record for this book is
available from the British Library

ISBN 978-0-00-822048-8 (hardback)
ISBN 978-0-00-822049-5 (trade paperback)

Printed and bound in Great Britain by
Clays Ltd, St Ives plc

MIX
Paper from
responsible sources
FSC™ C007454

FSC™ is a non-profit international organisation established to promote
the responsible management of the world's forests. Products carrying the
FSC label are independently certified to assure consumers that they come
from forests that are managed to meet the social, economic and
ecological needs of present or future generations,
and other controlled sources.

Find out more about HarperCollins and the environment at
www.harpercollins.co.uk/green

To my darling brothers, Alexis and Léopold
To my Granddaddy, whom I miss
And to every woman out there

It is the stars,
The stars above us govern our conditions.

Shakespeare, *King Lear*, Act IV, Scene III

Contents

Flashback

I DIDN'T WANT TO THINK about it any more. I was feeling fine, or at any rate better. Normal life had resumed: I was studying again, I'd moved into a new place, I'd found a boyfriend, a job and a future of sorts, and my figure was now more or less acceptable. I was increasingly thinking about getting into acting seriously, because in the end it was the only thing that genuinely interested me.

And then Mum called. 'Loutch, I've written an email to that MP who's trying to get a law passed on anorexia.' She wanted me to read it to see if I was OK with what she'd said and if I wanted her to include my contact details. I read it, and of course I was OK with it. And yes, I wanted her to include my contact details.

She sent it off, and then the journalists started calling with questions. So I told them my story, and everything started all over again.

The eating. Eating to fill myself up, to fill this void. Hating it, but doing it all the same. Seeing my body transform itself, even though I emptied it just as soon as I'd filled it. Not recognising it, and hating it. Not recognising myself, and hating me. Feeling so awful, so ugly and so empty. So like nothing at all.

And that's when I decided to relive, one final time, those eight months of my life spent suspended in a vacuum. To write it all down. To write about that constant spinning sensation in my head, that savage and brutal fear that used to devour my body and, to the extent that I still had one, my soul.

About the loneliness I felt when surrounded by all those cynics, the bastards, the lost and the miserable. About the unspeakably disgusting, skeletal ugliness in the midst of all that beauty. And about death itself, adorned in bright lights, make-up, fur, silk, rhinestone, lace, satin, soft leather and 7-inch heels.

The death that was very nearly my own fate.

Claudia Schiffer

IT WAS SUNDAY. Mum had practically dragged me out for a walk around the Marais district to take my mind off things. I didn't feel like it; I didn't feel like doing anything. I was revising for my Bac, the final year school exams in France, and the entrance exams for Sciences Po, France's leading political studies college, and as they loomed, my anxiety levels were rocketing. But mainly, I was brooding over my heartbreak. It was the first time my heart had been broken – by Hugo, who had just left me for Juliette. Dumped. Cast off like a useless, worthless object. The few words he'd said were like a slap in the face, a blow to the soul. A failure. Since then, I'd been hurting a lot, and had felt a bit scared too. Of being dumped over and over again, of being alone. Of not knowing what to do with my life, let alone with whom. Scared of the unknown, of getting it wrong, of maybe losing my way.

All of a sudden everything had become really complicated. After a 'problem-free' time at primary school, changes in the timetable cut me off from all my friends when I started secondary school. I completely stopped working and then I decided that I'd never set foot in a school again – I would prepare for my Bac on my own, at home. I planned everything out before announcing my decision to my parents: the contact details for a school where I could study by correspondence; my timetable, planned out to the minute, so that they could see that I really had thought things through; and my promise to do what it took to be the best.

My parents were hardly over the moon, but they agreed to it because they knew what I was like. I was a good pupil, I could put my mind to studying and more than anything I would never have let myself fail at something to which I'd committed myself. Especially when I'd just forced them into a corner. And I would pass my Bac, with a top mark.

It gave some structure to my life. I like to work fast; as soon as things start to drag, I get bored. I got the whole year's syllabus out of the way in six months so that I'd have time to do something else with the rest of the year. Like spending time with Granddaddy and Nan, my beloved grandparents. I learned how to dance the salsa and the tango and I also did a bit of acting. I hung out with my cousin Tom and his thirty-something friends, who used to take me out at night. And I spent time with my best friend Sophie, who I'd met at the dance classes. My life was very structured.

I'd get up at eight o'clock and at nine I'd settle down to work at my bedroom desk with Plume my cat for company, while Mum worked upstairs in her workshop. My mother is an artist – she paints, sculpts, makes collages and draws. She can put her hand to anything. And then it would be the lunch break, watching dumb serials on the box. Mum has never had much of an appetite and didn't stop for lunch. But I often went up to her workshop in the afternoons to spend some time with her, or we would go off to an exhibition or go shopping until the boys got back from school.

I've got two brothers: Alexis, who's a year and a half younger than me, and Léopold, who's six years younger. I used to feel happy when they got home. We'd have tea together in the kitchen, and life was peaceful and safe.

'No doubt about it – you're the next Claudia Schiffer.' We were window-shopping for watches in Rue des Francs-Bourgeois when a puny little guy accosted me. He hardly came up to my shoulders. I looked him up and down and he smiled at me. 'Have you ever thought about being a model?' Yeah, right, great chat-up technique. Thank you, and good-bye. But instead of ignoring him, Mum showed an interest. 'Your daughter is extraordinarily beautiful. She has a great nose! It balances her face and would catch the light perfectly. Believe me – I know what I'm talking about.'

He knows what he's talking about? When it comes to noses? I felt like laughing, because I know perfectly well what my nose is like. It's got a little bump, which has been handed down the maternal line in my family for at least three generations and which I spent my whole childhood rubbing, trying to flatten it out and make it go away. So much so that it's left a slight blue mark. Any true 'connoisseur' would know that what was not quite right about my face was my nose.

He addressed me informally as if we'd known each other for ever. 'I promise you, I know what I'm talking about. I work for a modelling agency called Elite. I don't know if you've heard of them? You were made for the profession, believe me. I could get you to New York for September fashion week, and you'd go down a storm. Here, take my card. Think about it, and call me. I promise you, you really are made for it. If you let me handle things, I can make you into a supermodel.'

I said thank you, but that I was revising for the Bac and for Sciences Po and none of this was on the cards.

'Just call me,' he said, and off he went.

Mum was looking at me with a big smile on her face. Once he was out of earshot, we burst out laughing. So they were true, then, these stories of scouts from modelling agencies accosting girls in the street and it all happening just like that, with a snap of the fingers in front of the window display of a jeweller's shop! Supermodel? Whatever next?

Mind you, Elite was a pretty big name. I might not have been a fashion addict, but I did read some of the women's magazines and I knew that Elite was one of the top agencies. A quick search on the internet that evening confirmed what I'd thought: Naomi Campbell, Cindy Crawford, Claudia Schiffer, Linda Evangelista ... Even though that Seb guy – the name Sébastien was on his business card – had gone over the top, it had still been nice of him to say that, just maybe, I could be part of that select band of the most beautiful girls on the planet!

It did me some good. I stored away Seb's card in a corner of my desk, and his fine talk in a corner of my mind, and plunged back into my revision. Deep down, I was trying to control the anxiety that gripped my stomach whenever I thought about the exams. I knew perfectly well that I would pass my Bac, and yet I was terribly afraid of failing it. As for Sciences Po, that was the great unknown. Not even my consistently excellent school grades were enough to set my mind at ease, and the closer the entrance exams got, the more petrified I became. I wasn't just fretting a bit – I was terrified of failing and proving that I just wasn't up to it.

Waiting for Sciences Po

I PASSED EVERY SINGLE ONE of my exams, with a warrior-like determination. I was quite the little trouper when it came down to it. The Bac was a cinch, but Sciences Po was another matter altogether. I stressed out crazily about not knowing a thing, about getting the one subject that I hadn't swotted up on. I'd prepared as best I could, but it just wasn't possible to revise the whole curriculum. I felt confident, as if I were in control of the situation, and yet at the same time I felt fragile and at the mercy of random chance, which could completely upset all my plans. The exam took place in a room without air conditioning where the temperature hit 40°C – it was an ordeal as much as an exam. And I wouldn't know if I'd passed it, or the other entrance exams I'd taken, until the end of July.

In the meantime, I decided to call Seb, just to see. When I asked him, 'Do you remember me?' he replied, 'I was hardly likely to forget you!' I know it was daft of me, but I liked hearing him say that. And after all, it was an option: if I wasn't smart enough to succeed with my brain – in journalism, theatre, politics or something like that – then perhaps I could use my 'dream body' to get on in life?

We set up a meeting and Mum dropped me off at his door near Saint-Michel. She must have said at least a dozen times: 'If there's the slightest problem, you leave, promise? And you call me. You call me and I'll come and get you.' Don't worry, Mum. I just wanted to talk about what the job entailed, find out how things worked and see what he had to offer me. Then if I didn't get into Sciences Po or one of the other colleges, there was still a chance of finding myself in New York for fashion week. I'd been dreaming of New York ever since *Friends* and *Sex and the City* and perhaps I'd take to fashion week really well.

This guy really talked nineteen to the dozen. He didn't stop talking from the moment I entered the room, going on about my nose, my blue eyes, my endless legs – 'How tall are you? Looking at you, I'd say 5 foot 10, right? Bang on, I knew it! You're just perfect, my angel. Perfect!' – as well as the agencies, the fashion shows, the castings, the photo shoots, the sublime clothes of the top designers, the ad campaigns worth hundreds of thousands of euros, the fantastic hotels all around the globe and all the top-flight models he'd personally discovered and coached to the summit of their profession. I politely listened to him taking me for an idiot. If he was so successful, what was he doing in this shabby little studio, which didn't even belong to him but to his girlfriend Clémentine, a pretty, slightly plump girl who wanted to become an actress and who he was 'coaching' too?

Being an actress was my own dream. I'd known it since I saw Romy Schneider in *Sissi* when I was 8. I'd taken the Sciences Po entrance exam because I was a conscientious pupil and my father had advised me to get some qualifications first, but my goal had always been to become an actress. 'You're mad, Victoire, don't even consider it!' Seb declared. 'You've got the physique of a model, not an actress. When I saw Marion Cotillard in *Taxi*, I knew straight away, before anyone else, that she would become a film star. She's got that something extra. You don't. You're a supermodel. You don't have a Hollywood face.'

He was increasingly getting on my nerves – all this talk about himself and the constant name-dropping. It smacked of lies, his whole spiel about being the African diplomat's son who'd wanted to study at Sciences Po (what a coincidence!) but had ultimately decided to 'coach his girls' instead. A pathetic mixture of fake bling, dreams and drudgery. But we were talking about Elite, after all, and he was saying he could get me in with them!

We did some photos, or rather 'Polaroids', as they're called – it used to be the only way they had of creating instant snaps. Nowadays, they're digital photos of course, but without any retouching or make-up or anything else, and he was going to use them to present me to Elite. In the *Vogue* magazines scattered on the coffee table, he showed me the basics of a pose: hair tied back to show off the face, head slightly inclined and looking straight ahead. 'Show intent in your gaze. We need to get the impression that you're thinking. And half open your lips, so that you don't look withdrawn.' One side of me wanted to take the piss out of him, while the other was concentrating like mad on trying to follow all his instructions at once. Seb was right: posing is a professional art. But did I really want it to be my profession?

When the time came to leave, I told him I would think about it.

My parents and I had a long discussion at home that evening. Dad was really into the idea: 'Do you realise what an opportunity this is, Victoire? You're going to be travelling around the world to the most beautiful places and earning loads of money for doing not very much. You won't get another opportunity like this. You're young, so you can afford to give it a go for a year.'

He was right: what if it was the chance of a lifetime?

But Mum was more hesitant: if I got into Sciences Po or one of the other colleges, was it really a good idea to turn them down? Of course what Seb was offering me was an amazing experience, but wouldn't I get tired of it very quickly, as I did with everything else? Wouldn't I regret it? Or, worse still, would I hold it against her and Dad for allowing me to make such a bad choice?

I went to bed with Seb's words whirling around in my head – all the magazine images he'd foisted on me, all the professional jargon he'd spouted and all the illustrious names he'd dropped into the conversation: New York, Tokyo, London; Polaroids, photo shoots, 'books', castings; Dior, Galliano, Céline, Castelbajac; Claudia, Natalia, Kate … If I didn't give it a go, would I spend the rest of my life regretting it?

The following morning, I called him: yes, I did want to meet Elite. Just to see.

Something Vintage, Something Classy

FROM THAT MOMENT ON, everything happened very quickly. It was already the end of June. At the start of August, I was off with Alexis, Léopold and my parents for a grand trip along the western seaboard of the United States to celebrate my parents' twentieth wedding anniversary, and the fashion week castings started at the beginning of September in New York. So I had barely a month in which to: get myself ready for meeting Elite, meet Elite, think it over, negotiate and sign a contract (or not), learn the techniques and the primary rules of the profession and get used to the idea.

Seb arranged an appointment for just three days later. 'I'd already spoken to them about you. When they saw the Polaroids, they said, "Bring her here immediately!"'

Immediately, fair enough, but not before I'd found my 'model's outfit': ultra-tight skinny black jeans to show off my legs to best effect; a black Petit Bateau tank top to flatter my top half, and then 'something vintage and something classy, that's what creates the magic balance, baby'. And so off I went with Seb to the Marais for a shopping spree. He picked me out a disgusting khaki jacket, which reeked of second-hand, but which he found 'subliiiime, exactly what we're looking for'. So what 'we' were looking for was this shapeless and nauseating potato sack to hide my curves? 'Trust me, it's what I do for a living. Just wait until we find the shoes – you'll see.'

For the shoes, we got the metro to Franklin D. Roosevelt on the Champs-Élysées and he led me directly to Balmain – it was the end of the sales, and we'd be able to find some 'bargains' for 'barely' €400. I'd never spent such a sum of money on shoes! I started browsing around the shop, thinking that he must have some faith in me if he was prepared to spend that much on a pair of shoes. He rejected all my choices and then triumphantly held aloft a faintly absurd pair of black patent leather sandals, featuring a complex jumble of zips and 7-inch heels. They were divine, but doubtless completely unwearable. I decided to give them a go nevertheless. It took a while to figure out how to get into them, but when I finally stood up to walk around, they turned out to be a thing of luxurious wonder! Contrary to all my expectations, they were actually quite comfortable. And even if I'd have to get used to it, I was acquitting myself quite well at these vertiginous heights. After all, I'd spent years playing the little princess in shoes borrowed from Mum, who's always been very feminine and unafraid to wear high heels in the presence of my father, who is 6 foot 4. I'd never have believed it before trying them on, but Seb was right: these shoes were the touch of class and glamour that perfectly complemented my horrible military jacket. 'Shall I pay half, and your mother makes up the rest?' So nice of you, Seb, to get me just the one shoe! I only hoped my parents would be willing to chip in for this beautiful gift.

We got the metro again, me with my incredible sandals wrapped in silk paper and nestling in an understated little bag featuring the Balmain logo, and Seb in a growing state of excitement and issuing an incessant stream of instructions and advice about my appointment in two days' time at Elite. In a nutshell, I had to be smiley and relaxed and give the impression that I was pleased to be there. And above all, I had to let him do the talking and I had to make an amazing impression, because he'd spent days and days banging on about me and had managed to convince them that I was *the* supermodel of tomorrow. And the proof that he had managed to convince them was that a certain Flo, who only worked with the top-flight models, would be taking care of me and not Solène, who was in charge of the new faces. 'I want you to set off like a rocket, do you understand? I want you to get the best castings and the best fashion shows right away, without going through the "beginner" phase.'

I listened without saying a word, because that was what he seemed to expect of me. I was too well brought up to tell him that I was perfectly capable of taking all these instructions on board without him having to repeat them endlessly. I'd understood the basic deal, and even the finer detail, even though he had overlooked one crucial point that didn't even seem to have occurred to him: I hadn't yet decided if I would sign or not. Contrary to what he seemed to think, it wasn't a done deal. For a start, Elite had to be interested in me. And I had to be interested in them too.

Before I returned home to show off my combat outfit to the whole family, we stopped off at a café to see Olympe and Madeleine, two other 'Seb girls' he'd talent-spotted a few months previously and who I would be sharing an apartment with if I went to New York in September. I listened distractedly to the ramblings of our mentor, who was intending to turn us into the 'Galactic' (*sic*) superstars: three supermodels who would take the upcoming fashion weeks by storm. I listened a bit more attentively, but without really following everything, to his convoluted explanations about why he had decided (and what about me, when did I get to decide?) that in New York I would be represented by a small agency called Silent ('much more efficient and better organised') and in Milan by D' Management ('much better established than Elite in Italy').

The girls seemed nice. While Seb tucked into a huge *croque-monsieur* and downed Coca-Cola, I sipped on a freshly squeezed orange juice. My two (potential) flatmates were drinking Diet Coke. Seb was ribbing the girls about the lack of visible progress they were making with their respective diets: 'New York is in two months, girls. And by the looks of it, you're still a long way from a size 6.'* I was a long way from that too. Not quite as far away as they were, to look at them, but even so. What with splitting with Hugo and revis-

---

* Sizes given throughout are UK sizes.

ing for my exams, I'd lost weight – I could feel it when I put on my clothes. My size 8s were becoming a bit loose, but I'd never worn size 6! I was going to have to knuckle down …

That evening at home I told them about my 'Pretty Woman' day. I paraded in front of my parents and brothers in my Balmain sandals and my camouflage jacket, which I then washed in the machine several times to try to get rid of the mouldy second-hand smell. I almost forgot about my Bac results, which had come through that day: I missed the top grade by just 0.3 points due to a marking error in the sports exam. I was going to have to appeal, because without that top grade I wouldn't be eligible for the oral entrance exam for Sciences Po (which would give me a second chance to get in if I failed the written exam). I started to cry from fatigue, shame and anger. My father was certain that I would be given the top grade after my appeal and wanted to celebrate my results with a bottle of champagne which he had put on ice for the occasion, but I refused any kind of celebration. I was terribly disappointed and annoyed, and I wanted to forget all about it.

Before he went to bed, Alex came into my bedroom and we had a long chat. He never expresses his emotions, but I could sense that he was both very proud and very worried. Just like I was.

The following day, Seb paid for me to get my hair cut by 'his' hairdresser. This was a novelty for me, because from the year dot I'd always cut my own hair. And it was with this new look – which wasn't so very different from the old one, in truth – that I went to visit Granddaddy and Nan, who were not exactly over the moon about the adventure that was opening up before me. And yet my grandmother should have been happy for me – she had always been so elegant and when she was young she used to draw such pretty fashion sketches! She'd always loved fashion and even worked as a fashion designer before deciding to pack it in and look after her four children instead. But she was a lover of literature too, and she couldn't understand why I'd choose New York over trying to get into college. Granddaddy, for his part, was simply worried: his little Victorinette all alone in New York, surrounded by the sharks? Was it really a sensible thing to do? I reassured them as best I could before going home.

We were all very excited. Dad suggested eating out to celebrate. But if I wanted to become a model, I was going to have to forget about eating out. Seb said I was 'perfect', but the girls had made a point of saying that a size 8 was still much too much.

So we didn't go out to eat. I spent a sleepless night, and the next day I headed off to Elite.

The Cathedral of Fashion

I DID EXACTLY what Seb told me to do: skinny black jeans, black tank top, horrible khaki jacket, ballet shoes, and my Balmain sandals in my bag. My hair nicely done, no make-up at all and sweating profusely, all got up as I was in my 'model gear' instead of sporting the nice light dress which this early July heatwave called for. I met up with him at Saint-Michel and we jumped into a deliciously air-conditioned cab, where my body could get back down to a normal temperature. Seb spent the time drumming into me once again what he'd been repeating incessantly for the last two days: be natural, show willing, keep quiet and do what you're asked to do. Amen.

It was one of those wonderful Haussmann buildings on Avenue Montaigne, just next to the Plaza Athénée. In the coolness of the entrance hall, I sat down on a step to put on my shoes, which was a whole palaver in itself, what with all the straps and my feet all clammy and swollen with the heat. Seb was watching me with a hint of irritation. 'You're going to have to work on your technique, aren't you?' Once I was perched on my heels, it seemed like he only came up to my navel – he was the ridiculous one. The first challenge: to stabilise myself at this improbable height. I was tottering a bit, but managed my first steps without breaking the heels or my ankles. Another sidelong glance from Seb: 'Upstairs, you don't want to be tripping, do you? It's a minimum requirement, if you want to make a good impression.' Thanks for the confidence boost, that's just what I needed.

We took the lift up without a word. First floor, second floor, third floor – I felt the stress rising up my legs and clutching at my innards the higher we went. The door opened, and my heels sank into the thick, dark red carpet. There was polished wood panelling and, at the end of the corridor, a large elegant door bearing the same shiny golden plaque as on the façade, engraved with the word Elite in very sober and stylised black letters. Behind it, you could hear the hubbub of busy people. I had stage fright, like in the theatre just before walking on stage, when you can hear the buzz in the auditorium. Take a deep breath. Think of my parents and my brothers. Of Granddaddy, Nan and even Plume. Think about everything that makes me strong and makes me feel good. And go for it, like diving into the big pool.

We buzzed, and the door opened onto a rather spacious reception area. Seb nodded at the receptionist, who recognised him and smiled back. She ushered us in with a wave of her hand. I could feel my heart pounding furiously. We entered a huge, bright white room, with light streaming in through tall curtainless windows. In the middle stood a gigantic black table which people were milling around, speaking French and English in hushed tones, their eyes fixed on their computer screens and their phones stuck to their ears. On the right-hand wall, there was a bookshelf full of perfectly aligned books with names written in capital letters on their spines. And covering the walls there were hundreds of images in neat rows: first names, faces, silhouettes and measurements. These are the 'comp cards', which models use as super-size business cards. They're a sort of snapshot of who they are, with the contact details of the agency.

The place was stunning – I felt as if I were in a cathedral, a cathedral of fashion, beauty and luxury. And this was perhaps where, in a few moments' time, my baptism of fire was going to take place. I wanted them to take me on; I wanted to be a part of this amazingly big, bright, white world; I wanted a piece of the condensed and effervescent energy that this place exuded. Providing they liked me.

Nobody was taking any notice of us. We walked across the room towards a small brunette wearing big glasses who was sitting at the end of the table. Her voice was deep and carried authority. I focused on walking with a casual, self-assured air, trying not to tremble. Seb greeted the woman with a 'Hi, Flo,' and she turned towards me. It was all happening very quickly. Just before she replied with a 'Hello' and a big toothy smile – almost too toothy, in fact – I saw her gaze slide attentively from the top of my head to the tip of my toes, and then back up again just as attentively, until it met me full in the eyes. Still smiling, she said, 'Hello, Victoire.'

'Hello,' I replied, holding out my hand. She shook my hand, though I immediately sensed that a handshake was a bit out of place here.

And then she turned to her colleagues and loudly announced, 'Look over here, everybody! This is Victoire, the new girl! Look how beautiful she is!'

They all glanced across to size me up in their turn, said hello to me very politely and then returned to their business, as if I'd already left.

And yet I was still there, standing up to my full height of 5 foot 10 inches, plus an extra 7 inches thanks to my Balmain shoes, in front of Flo, who was sitting in her armchair and speaking to me politely but firmly: 'So, you'd like to work with us? How did you meet Seb? What do you do in life? Could you take off your jacket?' Phew! It was a huge relief to finally take off my horrible parka, which I'd been slowly dissolving in. Meanwhile, Flo was looking me up and down again. 'Would you turn round?' I felt like a cow at a cattle market. A piece of meat being scrutinised and weighed before being devoured. 'Perfect. I'm going to introduce you to Vladimir, and then you can go and do the Polaroids with Nicolas.'

Did that mean that they were taking me on? Without discussion or negotiation or anything? She had said the 'new girl' as if I were already part of the team. And weren't they even going to ask me for my opinion? Seb seemed to be in seventh heaven, as if he weren't in the least surprised. As if everything had already been decided, without me having had any say in the matter.

Flo introduced me to Vladimir, the short man with the nice smile and the Serbo-Croat accent sitting on her right. He was the 'head of the bookers' – the agents who are in touch with the casting directors and send the models to the famous castings and other appointments, and then negotiate and sign their contracts. He greeted me with a 'My darrrling, how beautiful you are. Come along, I'm going to intrrroduce you to the boss.' I followed him towards an immense room with huge windows that gave onto a massive balcony overlooking the Avenue Montaigne. In the middle of it was an enormous black desk, behind which was sitting the only man in the whole agency who was wearing a suit and tie. 'Gérrrald, let me intrrroduce you to Victoirrre, the new girl.'

He looked up at me. 'Hello, sweetie.'

'Hello.'

And he buried his nose back in his papers.

Leaving his office, his 'sweetie' was asking herself what she was doing there and if she really wanted to get mixed up with all these people, who were seemingly from another planet.

Nicolas, a very thin and very agitated young man, closed the large doors to the boss's office so that he could photograph me in front of them. A first profile, a second profile, from the front, from the back, hair swept back over the ear. I remembered what Seb had told me two days earlier: a look of intent in the eyes, head slightly lowered, lips half-open.

Once the Polaroids were done, we went to the other end of the corridor, where a very cool-looking woman – huge trendy glasses, black jeans, big-brand trainers and immaculate hair-cut – greeted me without a smile and without introducing herself. 'Walk!'

I did as I was told, putting as much grace into it as I could. 'Again!'

Going down the corridor for the second time, I tried to catch her eyes, but she was staring at my bottom, not my eyes. At my arms and my legs. The less she said, the more I felt I was moving like a robot.

'OK. You're going to have to take walking lessons.'

Walking lessons? Did such things exist? I was about to come up with a reply, when I realised that she wasn't talking to me but to Seb. Still without addressing me directly, she took a tape measure out of her pocket and came over to take my measurements. Chest, waist and hips, or rather the fat of the buttocks! I sensed that it was a crucial moment, but I had no idea what score I needed to pass the examination. '34, 25, 36.' Was that good or not? Seb said nothing.

Flo appeared and asked, 'Well, then?' The figures were repeated to her. She sighed. 'OK, we'll lie, because you're never going to get into the clothes – you absolutely have to be close to 34. We'll put 34 and reduce the rest too. In any case, it's eight weeks away and you'll have more than enough time to lose it.' She looked at me, giving me another of her toothy smiles. She was smiling, but in reality she wasn't smiling. She was giving me a very strict order. 'For the photo shoots, size 8 is fine and you can put some back on. But for the shows, you have to get into size 4 to 6. OK?'

OK.

Before we left, Vladimir asked me to sit down at his desk – what a relief it was to finally take the weight off my feet! – and handed me a contract in a classy white sleeve engraved with the Elite logo. He also reeled off a list of the things that I needed to do as a priority: sign the contract in question, do a photo session with one of their photographers so that they could print my comp card and put together an initial portfolio, and arrange walking lessons. 'You're rrreally too beautiful, my darrrling. Do a good job in New York. We'll be seeing each other again for Parrris fashion week.'

We signalled goodbye to Flo, who was on the phone, and found ourselves back in the lift. Sébastien, who had never been so silent in all the time I'd known him, became Seb once again: I'd been great, they'd been amazed, he'd done the right thing to make sure that it was Flo who took me on, he'd negotiated like crazy but it had worked, and thanks to him I was going to have an incredible first season and become the supermodel who everyone wanted a piece of, because when 'they' find a French girl, 'they' never let go. The French girl is the must-have, and there aren't so many of them on the market – perhaps two or three. 'And one of them is you! You'll see. In New York, Milan and Paris, it's *you* they're all going to want!'

So that was it, it was a done deal? In the entrance hall, as I extricated my feet from my sandals from hell, I felt drained and dazed, excited and out of myself. All these people had chosen me, appraised me, measured me and given me a schedule without once asking me for my opinion. Perhaps it was better that way. I wasn't sure that I had an opinion. My life was in the process of taking off, without me really having had any say in the matter. And so what? Perhaps that was how life worked? Going with the flow and letting life take decisions for me? Letting it take me wherever it wanted to take me? Ultimately, there was nothing I had to do personally, except do what I was told and do it to perfection in order to become the best. And stop eating, straight away.

Mum was waiting for me in her old Austin Mini on the Avenue Montaigne – getting the metro in this heat was more than I could face. 'So, what did they say, then?'

I gave her the low-down. Flo, Vladimir, Gérald, the contract, the Polaroid session, the walking lessons and the measurements.

'An inch around the hips is quite a lot, Loutch. You've never been so slim, and you've got an iron will!'

She was right. But I was going to become a supermodel, the supermodel who everybody wanted a piece of. I was going to have a dazzling rise to the top, earn loads of money and kick off my adult life in an incredible way.

I had just turned 18, Elite thought I was terrific, and in September I'd be in New York! When I got home, I weighed myself. At 5 foot 10 and weighing 58 kilos, I could get into a size 8. So I'd need to lose at least three 3 kilos to reach size 6, and three more to get to size 4. It was 2 July and the first castings in New York were starting at the beginning of September, so I had eight weeks to reach a weight of 52 kilos.

Or let's say 50, so that I had a bit of leeway. That meant a kilo a week, which I should be able to manage.

I spent the rest of the evening on the internet, browsing sites and blogs by girls who offered slimming tips. It was pretty straightforward, in fact: I would just eat fruit. And more specifically, apples, because the pectin in them makes you feel full. I'd eat them three times a day, chewing tiny pieces very slowly, like Mum does when she eats a *pain aux raisins*. It was the same as preparing for my Bac or the Sciences Po exam: I just had to remain focused on my objective. I'd done it before and I could do it again. It shouldn't be a major obstacle – it was just a question of willpower. And I had plenty of willpower.

Playing With My Body

TWO DAYS LATER, Mum dropped me off in front of the grimy old façade of a disused shop in the 10th arrondissement. I checked twice to make sure that this really was the address where I was supposed to meet Seb for my first photo session, tapped in the code and pushed open a rickety door which gave onto a dimly lit staircase with a grubby carpet. I very nearly turned around and left. It was quite a contrast to the agency on the Avenue Montaigne! At the bottom of the stairs, I came to a dark and cluttered room. At the far end, in front of a large mirror, there was a small table piled high with dirty clothes and a heap of spent make-up tubes. Syringes and used condoms were scattered across the filthy floor. What was I doing here?

A smiling Seb appeared in the frame of a little door hidden off to the side in the shadows, accompanied by a sort of hairy giant whose huge belly was spilling out of a T-shirt that was much too small for him. No need to panic. Mum knew where I was and I could call her at any moment. Plus, I knew Seb and it wasn't in his interests for anything to happen to me.

Seb introduced me to Sergei the photographer, who took hold of me as if I were a rag doll and planted a huge kiss on both my cheeks. I felt myself relaxing – the guy was a big teddy bear, who spoke English with a Serbian accent you could cut with a knife. He told me I was 'wonderful', that he was 'so happy to have the honour' of doing my very first photo session and that I had nothing to worry about, because we were going to have 'so much fun together'. He led me into his studio, which was a large, very brightly lit room with a huge roll of something that looked like white paper hanging from the ceiling and spiralling down to the floor, partially covering it. The light cast by two large projectors was both soft and bright. It was exactly what I'd imagined a photo studio might look like.

Seb was pleased to see that I'd followed his instructions to the letter: skinny jeans, shirt and denim jacket. Sergei politely asked me to take off my jacket and my bra, pointing to an adjoining room where I could get changed. When I returned, he came over to me and in a very considerate way said, 'Can I?' I nodded and he undid several buttons of my shirt. I felt both embarrassed and at ease – I could sense that he respected me.

During the two hours that the session lasted, Sergei always asked permission before touching me – each and every time. He asked me to move into the middle of the paper, which was in fact a kind of very luminous fabric, got behind his camera and said, 'OK.' Yes, but OK what? I had no idea what he was expecting of me. And so, patiently and kindly, he explained and guided me through things in his Anglo-Serbian jabber. I needed to relax. To put my weight on one leg to get a sway into my hips. To lower my head and raise my eyes. To play with my body.

Playing with my body – what a strange experience it was for me! I was 18 years old, with a woman's body but the outlook of a well-behaved little girl. That was no doubt why Hugo had left me – after a few weeks of gentle smooching and lengthy and passionate conversations about literature, his hand crept a bit lower than my breasts and a bit higher than my thighs. He sensed my reticence: it was the first time a boy had touched me like that. I wasn't ready, or even sure if I wanted to be. He said that it wasn't a problem, that we'd take our time and that he'd be patient. The following week, he was gone. That was where I was at with body games when Sergei tactfully started encouraging me to be 'more sexy, baby', to open my shirt, undo my trousers, prostrate myself languidly on the floor and surrender myself up to his lens. I went along with it and let him do what he wanted to do, because he was extremely kind and professional.

He enticed me into playing the game. The less tense my body became, the more I started to enjoy myself. 'I love it, darling. Wonderful! Look up for me! Look down for me! Give me more, baby!' I swung my hips, ran my hands through my hair and crawled around like a cat in front of his lens, looking into his eyes. I changed my outfit, opened my shirt, undid my trousers. I struck the poses and began to under-stand the rules a little. I forgot all about Seb and just had a good time with Sergei. It was novel, funny, sexy perhaps, but without being sexual, surprising, strange and exciting …

Seb congratulated me on the session. 'You did very well, but next time it must be a flesh-coloured thong and bra. That's one of the basics of the profession. Underwear you can't see, even in see-through clothes.'

There was no way I could have known that, but I should at least have thought of wearing some lingerie that was half-way presentable. The shame when I took off my jeans and realised I was wearing the tattiest pair of knickers in my whole pantie drawer!

As I was leaving, Sergei took hold of me again and planted a big kiss on both cheeks. I deployed my best English to thank him for having been so sweet and so delicate with me. 'Good luck, Victoire, and thank you for this beautiful moment.'

After this brilliant photo session, time seemed to speed up. There was no time to see Sophie and tell her about my adventures as a future global muse or hear about her trials and tribulations as a future student of journalism, or to spend an evening with cousin Thomas. I was booked for the fashion week in New York at the start of September, the one in Milan at the end of September, and the one in Paris in early October. If I'd understood correctly, in each city the idea was to do as many castings as possible during the first week and hope to be chosen for the fashion shows in the second week. If I was lucky enough to get noticed, after the fashion weeks I might be chosen to do photo shoots for the magazines, for all the catalogues of the brands and even – joy of joys – for one of their ad campaigns. That was the ultimate goal: to be chosen for a campaign, to become the face of a brand and to be paid a fortune for it.

While waiting for glory, and before flying off to the States with my family on 11 August as planned, I still had to arrange a couple of walking lessons, an appointment with Dad's lawyer friend to go through the contract, a meeting at Elite to sign the contract and take possession of my book and my comp cards, and another one with Silent, the agency that would be representing me in New York. I had to do all that before heading off in the last week of July and the first week of August to Marseille, where we'd be joined by my grandparents at the lovely house with a swimming pool belonging to some friends of my parents.

I had also planned to spend three days in London with Alexis to honour an appointment I'd spent weeks trying to arrange and which I couldn't bring myself to cancel, even though it didn't seem very relevant any more. Being an actress had always been my dream and one day I'd make it come true. I had got it into my head to meet the agent of Robert Pattinson, who was my favourite actor at the time. His agent was a certain Kate Staddon, whose contact details I had found on the internet. I desperately wanted to talk to this woman about the options available to me for making it as an actress in England. I'd harassed her office every day for nearly a month until they were forced to give in to the inevitable: the easiest way of getting shot of this French girl was to agree to meet her, even if it was only for fifteen minutes.

And so Alex and I headed off as planned for a little trip to London, where we stayed with his godfather and took in the pubs, parks and museums. This sibling escapade did us good, or it did me good anyway, coming as it did just before all these big changes in my life, and so in the life of our family too. We spent a long time talking about the events of recent days, and when I told him about my session with Sergei, he asked me: 'Would you be capable of posing naked?' I was completely unable to answer him, but we were in agreement on one point: if I ever did, it would be best if Dad never saw the photos. But above all, we took full advantage of our time in London together, exploring new parts of the city that we weren't familiar with. On the day of my appointment, my brother accompanied me to the door of the agency and then stationed himself on the pavement opposite to wait patiently for me.

Kate Staddon was charming. She told me that, in addition to being rather tenacious, I was really very pretty, but that nevertheless my only chance of becoming an actress in the United Kingdom was to knuckle down at one of the leading drama schools, where she advised me to spend several years doing a course in order to obtain a suitable qualification. And when I'd done that, she'd be happy to see me again to discuss my future. I thanked her profusely. I had understood her message loud and clear: theatre directors didn't cast their actors by hanging around in the street. They audition professionals who know their trade because they have learned it, though perhaps they bumped into supermodels on international tours occasionally and suddenly felt a burning desire to cast them in a role in order to reveal their hidden talent? And supposing that never happened, perhaps those very same supermodels, after two or three years of modelling, would have amassed enough money to enrol in one of those fantastically expensive drama schools that Kate Staddon had mentioned?

When I explained all this to Alex on the way to St Pancras to get the Eurostar back to Paris, where my walking lessons awaited me the next day, he listened to me attentively and indulgently. And then simply said, 'Vic, don't let yourself dream too much, will you?'

Learning How to Walk

SEB HAD TOLD ME that she was a former model. According to him, he was paying for a session with walking teacher Évelyne (€150 an hour) because she was the best person to teach me how to walk the catwalks, on which I was supposed to be parading in a few weeks' time with perfect ease and with that feline allure that their name suggests. 'Don't forget your Balmains, otherwise it'll be pointless.' And so there we were, Mum and I, standing in front of the door of an apartment on the thousandth floor of a dizzying tower in the 12th arrondissement. The woman who opened the door to us didn't look like a model at all: her feet were bare, her grey hair was held up in a messy bun by her glasses, she was wearing a colourful silk djellaba and her fingers were bedecked with silver rings. She gave us a friendly welcome and ushered us into a purple, orange and pink apartment full of Buddhas, candles, Indian wall hangings, rugs, embroidered cushions and a faint but pervasive smell of incense.

She offered us some tea, pushed all the furniture in the living room against the walls to create a corridor for walking, and installed Mum on a chair so that she could observe everything, remember anything I might forget and then help me practise during the holidays in order to be ready for New York. I put my hair up in a ponytail, slipped into my performing sandals and off I went. She immediately saw that I knew how to walk in heels – 'You have the grace of Lauren Bacall' (isn't she a Hollywood star, Seb?) – but that I was holding myself too erect, a bit like a classical dancer, and that I was much too tense.

She showed me how to relax my shoulders and arms, right down to my nails, with a few little exercises. We spent quite a while on the issue of 'Playmobil hands': how to make sure that I didn't resemble a Playmobil figure with stiff arms and hook-like hands. And so I learned how to think about relaxing my fingers when walking. And also how to swing my pelvis to relax my legs and to inject movement into my arms, how to lower my head slightly while looking up in order to obtain that 'killer look', how to erase any kind of expression from my face – 'Above all, never smile!' – so that I would look superior and detached from the humdrum world, and how to concentrate on always walking in a straight line. And of course she also showed me how to adopt that ridiculous gait that is peculiar to models: one foot placed exactly in front of the other with a high knee lift and a big stride, which makes even the most beautiful of creatures look completely stupid. 'It's a convention, Victoire, and you have to master it. Never forget that they're looking at the clothes, not you.'

After an hour of this, I was knackered. 'Practise a bit every day. You'll see, your body will internalise it all and you won't even need to think about it any more.'

In the lift back down to earth, it occurred to me that not even a month ago I'd been completely immersed in revising. And I couldn't help wondering if I really wanted to spend the rest of my life focusing my energies on crucial issues like 'Playmobil hands'. We were a long way from Shakespeare and global geopolitics!

The question of the contract still had to be dealt with, and I was reassured that Dad was taking care of it. I knew that he would do what was in my best interests. I went with him to see his lady lawyer friend, who explained that Elite would be looking after me in France; Silent, who I had not yet met, in New York; and D' Management, who I would be meeting in Italy in October, in Milan. All these agencies negotiated each of my individual assignments, charged a fee to the clients, kept a percentage of these fees and paid a small sum to Seb, who remained my 'primary agency'. All my expenses would be advanced to me and the agencies would reimburse themselves at the end of the season from my earnings.

When I asked Seb why Elite couldn't represent me all around the world, he got into convoluted explanations about how in New York and Milan the small agencies had much more clout than a big machine like Elite and that they would be much better placed to look after me. My job was to make them want me, and if I placed my trust in him, he knew this world like the back of his hand and knew better than anyone what would be best for me. And for him too, no doubt, though I didn't say that to him.

He was increasingly getting on my nerves with his incessant chatter – the mere thought of him opening his mouth tired me out. But I decided to trust him. When it came to the important things, he'd made good on his promises: he had indeed introduced me to Elite and had made sure that I went straight onto the roster of top models managed by Flo. He'd paid for my sessions with Sergei and Évelyne, who were just the type of professionals I needed. And above all, he would be in New York with me when I took the big plunge.

It was the first time in my life that I was going to travel somewhere without at least one member of my family. I was trying not to think about it too much, but it was making me really anxious. The fairy tale would have been perfect if Mum could have come with me, but Seb had made it clear that this was not on the cards. And anyway, if Mum came with me, who was going to look after the boys? In September, Léopold would be entering Year Eight and Alexis Year Twelve, and so it was important for her to be there for them. I was the big sister and I had to learn how to fend for myself, and so I was very happy in the knowledge that that pain in the neck Seb would be by my side to guide me through this alien world.

Naturally it was Seb who took me to see Silent a few days before I left for Marseille with Mum. Rather than receiving us in their offices, they asked us to come to a photo studio in the suburbs where they put together the images and videos that they use to promote their stable of models. And so the meeting took place on the top floor of a warehouse, which you accessed via a goods lift. How cool! Everyone was quietly busying themselves in this rather grand loft space, which was like a well-ordered beehive. In one corner there was an open kitchen with a well-stocked buffet which Olympe and Madeleine were busy nibbling away at. I greeted them with a smile. In another corner, between two bulging clothes racks, there was a sort of dressing room where the girls were getting their hair and make-up done. I immediately recognised the very beautiful actress Emmanuelle Seigner, who was getting a blow-dry. Technicians and assistants were beavering away in a huge empty space that was surrounded by projectors and all the photographic and video paraphernalia.

Seb introduced me to Louis, a tall elegant man with a piercing blue gaze who was wearing a pristine shirt and perfectly tailored trousers and was casually sockless in his smart shoes. He was one of the founders of the agency. He greeted me as if he'd known me for ever and hadn't seen me in ages: 'Ah, Victoire, I'm so happy you're here! You know, we're so pleased to be taking you to New York with us. We're going to do beautiful things together! Have you met Émile?'

He led me over to his partner, who was at the buffet. He had a nice-looking face, was slightly too tanned, perfectly shaved, had very white teeth and was wearing a rather crumpled linen suit and a pair of flip-flops. It was another kind of elegance, which jarred somewhat with the way he spoke: he was in the process of giving Olympe and Madeleine, who hadn't moved an inch from the buffet, a dressing-down. 'For fuck's sake, girls, you have to know what you really want! We'll be in New York in six weeks, and you go on eating regardless. Stop eating! We're not going to take you there in that state.'

I felt embarrassed for them and I could see that they were furious that I was witnessing this scene under Seb's satisfied gaze. But above all, I found it unfair: they were perfectly slim. I wasn't sure I would be able to do any better.

For the time being, the apple diet was working: I'd weighed myself that morning, and I was touching 56 kilos. And I wasn't even really hungry! Amid this whirlwind of preparations, the fact was that I didn't really have time to think of eating. But would I hold firm over the long run? And why had they ordered this gargantuan buffet for a gathering of models who were all supposed to be on a diet?

Émile greeted me very sweetly too and introduced me to Nicolas, the hairstylist who was going to look after me. They were absolutely insistent on having me in the photos and videos that would serve to showcase the agency in New York. And so before I could blink, I found myself being made up and having my hair done all in one go. They took possession of me and all I had to do was let them get on with it.

Nicolas was in ecstasy about the quality of my skin: 'Wow, Victoire, you remind me of Daria Werbowy. And I know what I'm talking about, I did the Lancôme campaign with her.' I was flattered. For the last fortnight, I had been browsing through the magazines to familiarise myself with this new world and I'd spotted this sublime, blue-eyed brunette who, according to the papers, was one of the ten highest-paid models in the world. Let's hope that the comparison would bring me luck. 'Everybody will just adore a complexion like that! And you're right for every type of hair and make-up.'

He explained how it worked: a few days before each fashion show, a model is assigned to the make-up artists and hairstylists, and they use her to create the make-up and hairstyle look for the season. 'After that, they take Polaroids which are posted up in all the dressing rooms so that the other make-up artists and hairstylists can reproduce the look on all the other models in the fashion show.'

I didn't even have time to ask Nicolas if Daria was nice, because it was now my turn to be filmed. An assistant put me in front of the camera and a huge fan started up, sending my hair, which Nicolas had taken great pains to style, flying all over the place. 'Go ahead, Victoire! Walk around, use the space, enjoy yourself! Look at me. That's it! Now to the left. Your eyes, give me your eyes! Great! Laugh! That's perfect, we're done!'

It had been short, but intense. And I loved it!

Louis and Émile came over to say goodbye. 'We'll see each other again in New York very soon. Between now and then, get plenty of rest. We want you at the top of your game. And don't whatever you do get tanned! Stay in the shade – that's a must.'

In the taxi on the way back – thanks, Seb, for sparing us the train – my 'primary agency' insisted on this point: white skin, face and body. A tan was out of the question, and no bikini line either. And especially no muscles. 'Don't be doing any sport, will you? They want feminine women, not athletes.

The only exercise you're allowed is walking. You even need to watch it with swimming – wide shoulders are not attractive.' I couldn't help looking at him with a certain annoyance. 'Well, what did you think, honey? Being a top model takes effort! It's a profession.'

That same day, Vladimir, the head booker at Elite, took my parents out to lunch at L'Avenue, a chic restaurant on the Avenue Montaigne. No doubt Dad's constant calls about each little detail of the contract had started to irritate him. He'd probably decided that it would be easier just to speak to my parents directly and also get to know them a bit in order to put their minds at rest. They must have been used to that at Elite – I was almost old for a debutante. Most of their recruits were not even over 16 and I assumed that coaching the parents was also part of their job. Be that as it may, the contract issues were sorted out and my parents seemed reassured when they saw how serious the agency was about looking after me: 'In any case, it's in their interests that no harm comes to you. We trust you, but do be careful, Sweetpea.'

I don't think it ever occurred to Vladimir to invite me to this lunch too, which was fine by me, because there wasn't much for me to do in a restaurant. As somebody who worked in the industry, he knew that you didn't invite a model out to eat.

33 23 34

I RETURNED TO AVENUE MONTAIGNE accompanied by Seb to drop off my contract and pick up my book and my comp cards. It was Vladimir who greeted me with a wink and pointed to the wall of photos behind him: in the midst of all those other faces, I spotted mine. It took me a moment to realise that this girl, who looked every inch a model like all those girls in the magazines, was actually me. What a strange feeling it was! It was as if I could recognise my outer shell, while knowing perfectly well that it wasn't me inside. I sensed it was going to take me a while to get used to my new image: of me the model ...

The book made an even bigger impression, when I saw Sergei's photos for the first time. The sexy girl in the oversized shirt was me! The one whose breast was peeping out a bit (I wouldn't be showing that one to my father), the gentle dreamy one in front of the mirror, the one with the killer look ... All of them were me. On the comp card, slipped into the back of the book, it said: 'Victoire Maçon Dauxerre, 5'10", 33–23–34, brown hair, blue eyes', complete with the smart Elite logo.

I left feeling a bit dazed, with my comp cards and contract in my bag. A month previously, I was a totally stressed-out girl about to take the entrance exam for Sciences Po, and a month later, I was a totally stressed-out girl who everyone thought was a super-sexy woman and who was on her way to New York fashion week.

The night before we left for Marseille, I went to the cinema with my parents to see *Picture Me*, a documentary by Sara Ziff, an American model who had filmed her life over the course of a year. She recounts the happy times – the fashion shows, the adorable designers, the incredible hotels – but also the harsh side of this profession: the endless waiting at the castings, the occasional cruelty of the people who dress you, style your hair and do your make-up, the rivalry between the girls, the disjointed lifestyle, the jet-lag, the pressure and the feeling of being treated like an object, or sometimes worse than an object.

As I came out of the cinema, a man came up to me: 'Excuse me, Mademoiselle. Have you ever thought of becoming a model?' I was so taken aback that I didn't know what to say! He introduced himself, said that he worked for a major agency and that, if I was interested, he would be happy to … I laughed as I told him that I had just signed with Elite. 'I'm out of luck, they were quicker off the mark than me! I wish you a wonderful career.'

In the car on the way home, my parents spoke very frankly: the film clearly showed that it was a profession that could be very brutal. They stressed that I should never forget that I had a free choice and that I could decide what I wanted to do and what I didn't want to do. That I should never put up with people treating me badly. That they would always be there for me, and that I could call them at any time of the day or night. 'Well, preferably in the daytime, actually.'

Dad was trying to make light of it, but deep down inside I could feel something electric rousing itself in the pit of my stomach. The same thing that had stopped me sleeping before the Sciences Po exams. In fact, it was something I'd been familiar with for virtually my whole life. It was a stabbing anxiety that implanted itself in my guts and then wouldn't let go. The same anxiety that had made me ill at primary school, that had stopped me returning to secondary school and that demanded that I be the best at everything all the time, so that people would choose me, love me and stick with me.

It was that bastard fear. That evening, I felt it stirring within me. And I realised that it would be my sole companion when I set off for New York.

Three Apples a Day

MUM, LÉOPOLD, MY GRANDPARENTS AND I left for Marseille. Dad was due to join us the following week, while Alexis had decided to go to the Bayonne festival with his friends instead. And so there we were on holiday in a pretty villa and the only thing on the agenda was to enjoy ourselves and each other's company. Well, not quite, because I did have a bit of 'holiday homework'. For a start, Seb and Flo had both insisted that I swot up by reading the fashion magazines and taking note of the postures and faces of the models and the names and styles of the designers, the make-up artists and the hairstylists. That way, I'd get a better idea of what was expected of me. Then I had to practise walking according to Évelyne's instructions: relax the facial muscles and the shoulders, think about my fingers in order to avoid the Playmobil arms, move my pelvis smoothly, focus on keeping straight, stare into the middle distance (for the killer look) and put one foot in front of the other like a big old horse. I performed all this by the edge of the pool, which made for a perfect catwalk, but only on the shady side to avoid getting tanned.

Finally, I had to continue to lose weight so that I could easily get into that famous size 4, which I hadn't even known existed before being spotted by Elite. Up until that point, I'd managed things impeccably: three apples a day, carefully selected on the basis of their appealing colour and appetising shape. Before each meal, I picked out a pretty plate and laid out the contents of my unchanging menu on it with ever-increasing artistry: in a mosaic, in a fan shape or cut into little dice or thin slices, all to be savoured slowly, biting into them and chewing well before swallowing. I also drank a few coffees, but not too many, and a lot of Pepsi Max (because it tasted better than Diet Coke and the bubbles made you feel full). I didn't drink anything else at all. For the first three days, I felt a bit hungry, but nothing I couldn't handle. And in the days that followed, I began to feel lighter and lighter and stronger and stronger, like a sportswoman pulling off a good performance. In the space of a week I had already lost nearly 2 kilos. Losing weight was quite easy, in actual fact!

But things began to get a bit complicated in Marseille. As I had nothing else to do but think about what lay in store for me, Flo's voice started to echo around incessantly in my head: 'Like that, you'll never get into the clothes.' This was just around the time that I was beginning to get fed up with apples. Sometimes I replaced them with other fruits, but how could I know what their exact calorie content was? Did half a melon or a punnet of strawberries contain more or less than an apple? On top of that, I had constant stomach ache. I didn't realise initially that eating nothing but raw fruit could cause these symptoms. I thought that it was the anxiety, because my fear had flooded into the vacuum and silence of the holidays, as if I'd opened the taps on a big pipe and a nasty, heavy anxiety was bubbling up inside me. And I had to fight hard to avoid drowning in it.

The results from Sciences Po finally came through: I'd failed. The doors to the other colleges were also beginning to close: I called Fénelon, Henri-IV and Louis-le-Grand to see if I could potentially postpone my starting date by a year. They said that I couldn't, but that there was nothing to stop me from reapplying the following year. This time, the die was really cast: I had no choice but to succeed in the path that fate had set me on.

If I screwed up in New York, I'd have nothing to fall back on.

Since I wasn't all that intelligent, the only option left to me was to be beautiful. I'd signed with Elite, and so I was going to be the best model in town. Impeccable, beyond reproach, utterly in keeping with what was expected of me. I was going to lose even more weight, learn to walk perfectly and do everything to ensure that my skin was an immaculate white. I was going to stack absolutely all the odds in my favour so that I would have a meteoric, explosive and dazzling career, because this was now my destiny, and it was up to me to grasp it by the horns.

So long as I managed to 'get into the clothes', obviously.

When, for the second day running, the scales stubbornly continued to read 52.9 and refused to go any lower, which they had been doing regularly since I'd started my diet, I cracked. I opened up to Mum, who always looked trim and sublime, no matter what. I'd never really broached the subject with her till then and she'd been watching me eating my fruit day after day without uttering a word. Naturally she did everything she could to reassure me: she told me that I was very beautiful, that I was already decidedly thinner than when they'd chosen me and that there was nothing to get worked up about, because I still had another month in which to lose that inch around the hips.

But I did go back onto the internet to look for some info on diets. All the websites talked about 'plateaux' – those times when, even if you stick strictly to your diet, your weight remains constant instead of dropping. If only I could have done a bit of sport, that would doubtless have helped me to get past the plateau, but all sport was forbidden. I did, though, permit myself a few lengths of the pool and I went to buy my fruit on foot so that I could get a bit of exercise – but only at the end of the day when the streets were in the shade.

It was the first time in my life that I hadn't spent the summer at La Baule. Every year from the year dot we'd always got together there with my grandparents. I loved their cute little house, nestling in a garden awash with lavender and a stone's throw from the beach. Granddaddy would take us shrimping and there was the smell of the sea and the seaweed. At teatime we would stuff ourselves on *niniches*, those long soft lollipops in all the colours of the rainbow, and large slices of brioche with redcurrant jelly, which was Nan's speciality. Or else a nice slice of buttered bread copiously smeared with *rillettes*. Granddaddy was a real food lover! When I was 10, they stopped renting that house and took a large seafront apartment instead.

I was the one who first noticed that Granddaddy was trembling. I remember it very well: it was the year I turned 13. I'd decided to interview him about his life story, because I admired him and I wanted to know everything about him. For several hours every day, he spoke into my microphone about his childhood and his youth. After studying at the École des Arts et Métiers, his dream had been to become a master glazier or else an art teacher and to take over the stained-glass workshop that his great-uncle had bequeathed him. But his grandmother had been firmly set against it. And so he set aside his dreams of being an artist and became an engineer and surveyor instead, always telling himself that once he retired he would take up painting, for want of stained glass. He drew wonderfully well, perfectly even. But when he finally did have the time for it, his hands began to tremble. In the space of a few months, his Parkinson's had put paid to his drawing.

That summer, Granddaddy had been too ill to enjoy the beaches of La Baule. And that was why we were now in Marseille, in this large, comfortable, one-storey house where he could get around more easily.

The more the days went by, the worse I felt. I was afraid of what lay in store for me, of not being up to it, of being separated from my family. And seeing Granddaddy in this state made me really sad. I loved him so much and I think we were very much alike in many ways. He knew about anxiety too and the fear of not being where you ought to be. Of passing the important things by, of not doing what you should have been doing, of missing out on the essential things, of failing in life.

As my father wasn't there, I slept with Mum. Right up against her to draw in her odour and her body warmth and to imprint the memory for when I was all alone over there and missing her terribly. I already knew that I would miss her dreadfully. Unbearably, even. I had no idea how I was going to get by without her and without the rest of them.

Even in the middle of the Marseille summer, tucked up in Mum's bed, I was starting to feel cold all the time.

Yùki

I MISSED SOPHIE, but I didn't dare ring her – I'd cancelled all the plans we'd had for July and we hadn't seen each other for ages. And what would I have said to her if I did ring her? That I was stressing out about the idea of going to work in New York, the city that I had been dreaming of for ever? That I wasn't sure if I wanted to become a supermodel, something that all the girls of my age dreamed about? That I was afraid of not being able to put one foot in front of the other on the catwalk and that I would have to make do with eating fruit while I was living out the dream? She had her own dreams of studying and becoming a journalist – what would she make of my little existential crises?

Fortunately, Léo was on hand to listen to me. Even though he was much younger than me, I'd always shared a lot with him. Whereas Alexis put me on edge with all his emotional stuff and intimate questions, Léopold listened to me very attentively and responded with tenderness and common sense. He would often say: 'You tell me about so many things that I'll be able to become a psychiatrist and I won't even have to study for it!' He was so cute when he explained to me that I was beautiful now and so there was just no way that, suddenly overnight, I wouldn't be beautiful any more. That I was too clever not to make a success of my new life. That I looked perfectly slim to him and he couldn't see what the problem was. That he was convinced that I would be taken on for all the fashion shows. And above all else, that I shouldn't worry, because what with Skype and texting and emails, we'd be able to speak to each other every day and they would always be with me. Nothing could separate us from each other, not even the 3,500 miles and the big time difference. 'And you know what, Vic? We really are all so proud of you. Not everybody has a supermodel for a sister. And at Elite, to boot!'

Dad eventually joined us. I did my best not to spoil the atmosphere, but I just couldn't shake off my anxiety. Happily, the scales finally deigned to drop again: I was slowly closing in on 51 kilos. So much so that Dad asked me if I was contemplating starting to eat a bit of meat and vegetables again. I think he just didn't get it. He'd always loved Mum and thought she was the most beautiful woman ever, but it had never occurred to him to wonder how she managed to stay so slim. The fact was that she had the appetite of a sparrow. I'd only ever seen her picking at food, never really eating. There was just no chance of her ever putting on weight. And in fact when Dad looked like he was going to insist on the meat and vegetables, she told him not to worry.

As the thing that scared me the most was the idea of being away from my family, I asked my parents to buy me a cuddly toy that I could take everywhere with me and would make me feel like I had them with me everywhere too. While they went off to look for one, Léo and I gave some thought to the name we could give it. As a lover of Asian culture, he explained to me that Japanese first names had actual meanings and so we went on the internet to have a look. That was a lot of fun. We ruled out Suki, which means 'love', Fuku, which means 'luck' but which didn't sound very appealing, and Kasoku, which means 'family'. In the end, we opted for Yùki, with an accent on the u. That means 'courage'. Léo said, 'That way, your courage will never fail you.' Leo really was so sweet and he was right, too: courage was exactly what I needed.

My parents returned with a cute little white rabbit, all soft and gentle, and I immediately adopted him. I sprayed Yùki with Mum's perfume and from that point on he never left my side.

We headed home from Marseille, Alex rejoined us, we packed our bags and we set off to the States.

The American Dream

I LEFT ON MY OWN a few hours before the rest of them on a different plane, because Silent had taken care of my return ticket. At the end of our family trip, I'd fly to New York from Los Angeles to get straight down to work and they would return to Paris. All of which meant that I was travelling with Air France and had been upgraded to business class like a star! I wondered if this was a foretaste of the new life that awaited me. The armchair that became a bed was a delight, as were the billion options available on my personal in-flight computer and the little complimentary beauty set. True luxury! And just as miraculous was the adorable air hostess who seemed to find it perfectly normal that I turned down my three-star meal in favour of fresh fruit.

I was in a bizarre state: both worried and excited, detached and nervous, grown-up and childlike. It was the beginning of adulthood for me, but I don't know what I would have done without Yùki there to comfort me.

I got a yellow cab to the hotel. Wow! New York! It was like being in a film, and not in the audience but on the screen: the taxi and all the smells, the car horns, the swarms of people all sweating profusely, Brooklyn Bridge, the Manhattan skyline ... I was in New York, New York! I was sure I was going to love it here.

As soon as my parents and brothers caught up with me, we began to explore every corner of the city. It was all set to be a dream holiday: New York, San Francisco, Las Vegas and Los Angeles, the five of us together and staying in incredible hotels. We'd been talking about it all year long and were so looking forward to it. And yet, though I didn't want to admit it, I was having trouble keeping up. I was absolutely knackered, almost certainly because of the jet-lag, which I just couldn't get over. And also because of that crazy month of July spent running around every which way, fretting over what choices I should make and what I was going to become, worrying about Granddaddy and trying to come to terms with my failure to get into Sciences Po.

And because of the fear, this constant nagging fear.

Traipsing around New York with the boys and Mum and Dad, I couldn't help thinking that in a fortnight's time I'd be here again, but all on my own. Central Park, the Guggenheim, the MoMA, Tribeca, Ground Zero, Broadway, the Rockefeller Center and the Statue of Liberty: everything that I'd always dreamed of was there within my reach, at my feet. Initially, it astounded me and then, all of a sudden, it overwhelmed me: I felt like I was losing my grip on the cliff face and that I was going to fall, and go on falling for ever. I didn't say anything to them about it so as not to ruin their trip.

One great thing here, though, was that the calories were marked on every item of food you bought. That way, I knew more or less what I was doing and it made up for the fact that I couldn't weigh myself, because there weren't any scales in the hotel rooms. I tried not to think about it too much. On the day I left Paris, my hip size was 35 inches and I weighed a teeny bit over 51 kilos. I absolutely had to lose at least one more kilo, but two or three would really set my mind at rest ...

Just a stone's throw from our hotel, there was an enormous store: Victoria's Secret. Mum knew that it was my dream to work for them. Who knew, perhaps in the not too distant future I would be one of their brand 'angels'? In the meantime, she took me there to treat me to some lingerie. I chose a very pretty black lace ensemble featuring a discreet little pink bow. A 'size 0' pair of knickers, which presumably corresponded to a size 34, and a 32A bra. It might have been bad news for me that I'd gone down two cup sizes, because personally I was fond of my breasts, but it certainly wasn't bad news for fashion week (I had of course noticed that many of the girls on the catwalks were flat-chested). I hadn't had my period either that month, no doubt on account of all the stress, but I wouldn't have minded it continuing that way – at least I wouldn't have that to worry about at work.

On the food front, Dad was starting to get annoyed. He was getting more and more insistent that I should eat some meat or fish and some vegetables. It drove me mad – that was my problem, not his. And if I'd started eating just like that, without being able to weigh myself, I'd have ballooned before I knew it. It was out of the question and so, as a compromise, we agreed that I'd eat out with them every other meal rather than all the time. So half the time I let them go off and have lunch or dinner while I found a nice piece of fruit or a low-calorie salad to eat on my own in peace and quiet, without having to endure my father scrutinising the contents of my plate all the time. You had to know what you wanted in life. He had been the first to encourage me to sign that contract and it was too late now to back away from the consequences.

When we turned in for the night, I cuddled up to Alex. All three of us slept in the same room – Alex and me in the double bed and Léo in the single bed. My brother didn't say anything, but I knew he could tell that things weren't OK. And I'd fall asleep clutching Yùki tightly and trying to convince myself that it would pass.

Three days after we arrived, we headed off to San Francisco. It was so beautiful taking off from New York just before sunset! Through the window, I watched the dazzling city recede, knowing I would be back there in a fortnight's time for the start of my new life. I felt the tears welling up in me and hid my face in my hair so that the others wouldn't notice.

Initially I hated San Francisco – it was so damn cold! What was the point of coming to California in the middle of summer if we were going to freeze to death! I felt tired and frustrated. I really could have done without spending the whole day wandering around the streets, which are so steep that you practically have to climb up them. I thought I was never going to manage it, constantly twenty paces behind the others and completely out of breath, as if I were on two packets of cigarettes a day. My parents started to lose their patience and Alex was actively sulking at having to wait for me all the time. My darling Léo walked right behind me, trying to chivvy me along: 'Come on, Vic, let's get into second gear!' I'd have loved to, my little Léo, but it was genuinely beyond me. I didn't know what was happening to me – I had no strength at all in my legs and I had a knot in my stomach. I was aching all over and my skin felt stretched to breaking point. I just wanted to go home.

Happily, the following day the weather was fine and warm and we travelled around on the streetcars. Not aching all over, and not feeling like a drag on everyone else transformed the whole experience. The more I got to know this city, the more I liked it. The colours, the very cool people, the flowers, the gardens, the beach and the blue, blue sea!

I was actually feeling better, and lighter. Lighter and lighter, in fact. Although it had to be said that the previous day had ended on a very bad note. Dad had insisted that I went to the restaurant with them and he'd also insisted that I ate some fish and vegetables. All right, they were steamed, but they came with a dressing too. I ended up giving in and I ate my fish and courgettes feeling like I was an ogre devouring thousands of calories. Alexis, who loves good food and can't bear public scenes, looked on aghast. And then I went to bed in tears.

After that, to try to calm my anxiety about eating, Dad had a brilliant idea: he bought me some scales. They were electronic and they were compact, so I could slip them into my suitcase and cart them around with me everywhere. I nervously weighed myself – it had already been a week since we'd been eating out in restaurants and hotels and I must have put on a good 2 kilos. And yet no, quite the contrary! I had even lost a little and was now just under 50! I weighed 49.8 kilos, to be precise. Of course you had to be wary, because scales often vary a bit in their readings. But overall, everything was fine and I could afford to relax a bit.

And so it was with a light heart that I agreed to dine out with them at a fish restaurant in the port. And I'm so glad I did! If I hadn't gone, I think I'd have spent the rest of the trip regretting it, because who should be sitting at the next table, but Douglas Kennedy! It was Dad who recognised him and I couldn't believe it, because I adored his books. I went straight over to speak to him and in my best English told him that I was French, that I loved reading his books and that I was so delighted to have run into him there. And he replied to me in French! He was absolutely charming and I was in seventh heaven. He signed an autograph and wished me good luck for the future.

Now I loved California and I loved the United States! I was sure my life here was going to be incredible.

We stayed for another two days in San Francisco and I really enjoyed being in the city, perhaps because my moods were like the streets there: they climb up and up and up, at the top of the climb there's a fantastic view of the horizon, you tell yourself this is paradise and that the world belongs to you, and then bang, the descent begins, you start tumbling down much faster than you climbed up and you find yourself in the bottom of a hole, which you have to extricate yourself from in order to start climbing again ...

The Little Voice

THE SCALES READ 48.9. I knew they were unlikely to be wrong, but I admit I didn't entirely trust them. When I looked at myself in the mirror before taking a shower, I could see that I still had a lot more fat to lose. This was obvious when I pinched the skin around my stomach and on my buttocks: there were folds of fat. And folds of fat were a no-no at fashion week. As the big day loomed, I could think of nothing else. A little voice, which was much more unpleasant than Flo's, had taken up residence in my head. No doubt it was the voice of my conscience, repeating to me on an endless loop: 'Stop eating, you're going to get fat. Stop eating.' If only I could have stopped eating, indeed stopped swallowing anything at all except for water and a bit of Pepsi Max, that would have taken care of virtually all my problems! Every time I ate, I felt like I'd failed. Almost as if my Sciences Po results were coming back to haunt me morning, noon and night.

We hired a car and set out on the road to Las Vegas and the northern end of the Grand Canyon. I've no idea how many miles we covered, but the drive seemed interminable.

The boys had brought loads of provisions with them and since there was nothing else to nibble on, I caved in and stuffed myself like a pig: two carrots, an apple and even a piece of chicken. I hated myself, I hated myself, I hated myself. Tonight the scales would no doubt be chanting in unison with my little voice: 'You're eating, you're getting fat, you're eating, you're getting fat …' Worst of all, when we got to the hotel I realised that there was not a single place where you could get hold of fresh fruit or unadorned steamed vegetables. Initially I felt really annoyed, but then it occurred to me that it was no bad thing, in fact; after everything I'd gobbled down in the car, the best solution was clearly to go on a diet.

I let them go off and stuff themselves with hamburgers and fries while I dreamed of spending all the money I was going to earn as a top-flight model on setting up a new restaurant concept that would be called Model Food. A calm, beautiful and immaculate place all in white with big, soft pink pouffes, as if you were in a cloud. The only items on the menu would be steamed chicken and fish, vegetables and fruits. Zero fat, zero sugar, 100 per cent purity and lightness.

The next day Mum and Dad had a surprise in store: we were going to a small aerodrome and would be flying over the Grand Canyon in an old crate with propellers, just like in the films. The boys couldn't contain themselves! I was excited too until I saw something dreadful in the hangar. As there were several of us and it was really a very small plane, everyone had to be weighed before boarding so that they could decide where everyone should sit in order to balance the weight properly. Weighing myself in public! My little voice immediately went mad. They were all going to see that I was too fat. Or too thin. No, too fat. The plane would fall out of the sky if I got on. It would never manage to take off and I would never manage to take off. I was a fat ball chained to the ground and I would never get off the ground, not for the Grand Canyon or for anything else in life. I didn't want to do it.

I really didn't want to do it.

Everyone else got on the scales, shoes, coats, bags and all. I didn't dare say to Mum that I didn't want to do it, so I handed her all my stuff so that I would weigh as little as possible. I concentrated as hard as I could so as not to see the guy looking at my weight, hearing him read it out and having to endure the moment when he said, 'Sorry, miss, not you.' But he didn't say a word and I got onto the plane with the others. And while everyone else was rhapsodising about the landscape, I spent the whole flight trying to shut up that bastard little voice, which was spoiling every second of the flight. And of my life.

When we got back to the hotel that night, I found myself briefly alone with Alex. He said that he'd had enough of it all; that they were spending all their time waiting for me, wrangling with me and hoping that I wouldn't throw a sulk and burst into tears; that even when I was there, I was absent; that he didn't understand what was happening to me, but that it was starting to get tiresome; and that I should do something about it. And then he turned on his heels and disappeared.

I knew that he was right and that he wanted to get a reaction out of me, shake me up and help me, but I just didn't have the strength to respond. I was feeling increasingly detached from everything, even from my own body. It was as if I could no longer connect with them or make them connect to me: we were all drifting apart. It was terrifying and there was nothing I could do about it. I was cold and aching the whole time, ever lighter and ever less substantial.

In reality, I was becoming less and less alive.

When we retired to our hotel room that evening, Alex looked me straight in the eye and said, 'I'm going to sleep in the little bed.' It was like a dagger in my heart. Even a big hug from Léo couldn't console me or bring me warmth.

Near Las Vegas we came across the most amazing outlet store I'd ever seen in my life: all of Ralph Lauren collections of the previous three years at 70 per cent off their usual American price! Dad said, 'Make the most it!' and we didn't need to be asked twice. There were loads of terrific things, all for next to nothing. I checked all the aisles for sleeveless tops, but everything, even the size 0s, was a bit too big. A very sweet salesgirl – American store assistants were always adorable – showed me a section where I might be able to find what I was looking for, and bingo! I found a short ivory jumper dress – the Irish sweater look – which was absolutely delightful and exactly my size. Matched with my splendid pair of Balmains,

I'd have the ideal look for the castings! The rack was full of little gems: I also found a tartan skirt and as many tops in 150–156cm as you could wish for. Pure bliss.

It took me a while to realise that I was actually in the children's section and that 150–156cm corresponded to age 12–14 back home. Which was a bit strange when you're 5 foot 10, but what was stopping me? That little dress was just perfect for me.

And I also found a pair of jeans. *The* pair of jeans, in fact. In the United States, jeans are an exact science: there's a measurement for the basic size, of course, but also another for leg length and a third for the width of the pelvis. It's very high-tech. After I'd tried a few pairs on, the salesgirl found me that rare pearl: a pair that was tight but not too narrow, so that I had a bit of leeway around the hips; long enough to go down to my heels; and nice and tight around the thighs. When I saw myself in the mirror, I was completely taken aback: was that slim girl with the endless legs really me?

The salesgirl's comment was: 'You are very skinny and so tall, with such long legs. Don't you want to be a model?' I smiled and explained that that was exactly what I was in the process of becoming and that next week I'd be in New York for fashion week. She looked at me with admiration and then asked, very shyly, if I would mind giving her my autograph. An autograph! Now it was my turn to be embarrassed. I thought about Douglas Kennedy, who I admired so much and who had been kind enough to sign an autograph for me a few days earlier in San Francisco. What a strange life I was leading! I attempted to react to this young woman with the same grace as he had, while wondering if I was an impostor or if she was a visionary.

That evening in the hotel bathroom, while the others were having dinner, I slipped on my jeans and took a photo of my figure, with my feet squeezed against each other so that I could see properly what I'd noticed in the store: I had a pretty thigh gap, like in the photos the girls posted on their dieting blogs. When I started my diet, that was the goal I'd set myself, and now I'd made it – I'd pulled it off!

I went onto the internet to check the French translation of 'skinny' and realised that I'd understood correctly. I also looked up the conversion tables for the American sizes and realised that I'd now hit the right sizes. Fantastic!

Now all I had to do was maintain this ideal weight: 48.5 kilos, according to my scales. In fact, I'd carry on down to 48, just to arrive at a round figure. A bit of roundness amid all this skinniness perhaps wouldn't be a bad thing! The only way would be to go on eating as little as possible, despite Dad's increasingly insistent and exasperated exhortations. When he bought the scales for me, he made me swear not to go lower than 52 kilos. I promised, but without knowing that I was already at 51. Since then, I was the only one who knew my exact weight, because it was the best way of keeping people off my back. I think Mum saw the reading on the scales at the aerodrome, but it was in pounds, not kilos. Around 110 or 108, or something like that: in those units, you feel like you weigh a ton! I wasn't sure if she'd bothered to do the conversion, but, either way, she hadn't mentioned it.

I had reached the perfect weight and the perfect size, but my mind wasn't at ease for all that. In fact, I was feeling ever more anxious. The closer we got to Los Angeles, the more my fear took over. Soon I would have to part with my family. Finding myself all alone in this big unknown world seemed ever more inconceivable as the moment approached. As I watched the surfers taking on the waves along the coast, it occurred to me that I, too, was going to have to remain standing on the crest of the wave, trying not to lose my balance and get dragged under. And on 7-inch heels, that was going to be no easy thing …

The day we arrived, we went to dine in Beverly Hills in the pretty villa belonging to Peter and Hemiko, friends of my parents. They were so lovely! Hemiko is a former model and she is ravishing. They have two adorable young daughters who looked at me as if I were the most beautiful thing on earth. We spent a really cool evening together, eating delicious fresh fruit and vegetables. As we were about to leave, Peter put his hand on my shoulder and said to me very kindly, 'You know, Victoire, if you don't treat the whole thing as a game, it's going to kill you. Keep your distance from that scene and don't neglect your private life – that's the most important thing. The agencies go out of their way to make you think that they're your family, because it's in their own interests. In actual fact, it's one big circus in which everyone is playing a role. Don't let them persuade you that your life hangs on the opinion of a single person! None of it is genuinely real or genuinely serious. Don't ever forget that.'

I immediately thought of Shakespeare, and the words of Jaques in *As You Like It*: 'All the world's a stage, And all the men and women merely players.' I don't know if that reassured or worried me. In any case, it did me good, because here was advice from somebody who knew what he was talking about.

Then Hemiko took me in her arms: 'Take care, and call us or come back if you need to. We are here for you.' That made me want to cry.

Stop Eating!

WHEN I WOKE UP on 25 August, I found a voice message on my mobile: it was the Lycée Fénelon letting me know that I'd been admitted onto their course. It felt like this call had come directly from another planet, but it gave me a boost all the same; even if it was no longer important, it meant that I hadn't failed at everything. I wondered if I would still be capable of knuckling down to studying. Thinking back to all the books I'd had to digest over the year to prepare for my exams, it scarcely seemed believable. Lately, I'd been having more and more trouble reading. I couldn't even manage the newspaper any more, as if something were preventing me from focusing my attention for more than three minutes at a time.

We spent the day cycling near Venice Beach. How wonderfully peaceful and beautiful it was! The people were cool and everybody seemed to be happy. The houses were stunning and looked directly onto the beach. The bodies were tanned, muscular and well-oiled. It was a gorgeous day, which I tried to savour as serenely as I could, while trying to forget the little voice that ever since the morning had been obstinately homing in on the anxiety of the moment: today, it was my parents' wedding anniversary. And that evening we were going to have to celebrate in a restaurant. 'How are you going to avoid eating? If you eat, you're going to get fat. How are you going to avoid eating?'

Oh shut up and move on!

But it was just as I'd been dreading: here was a menu four pages long and not a single steamed dish on it. There was some marinated mahi-mahi – a really tasty and non-fatty fish that I loved. But what was it marinated in? Apparently in lemon, ginger and spices, but they always forgot to mention that it would be swimming in oil too. Or else they'd add a 'little sauce' full of sugar. 'Don't worry about that – you can just take the marinade off,' was Dad's helpful suggestion. But I was worried, because even if I took it off some of it was obviously going to remain in the flesh – the whole point of a marinade was that it permeated the food and you took in the calories, even if you didn't eat the sauce. I couldn't make up my mind and really didn't feel like having anything at all. And because I was hungry, it was even worse: the fundamental failure wasn't eating, but feeling hungry. Given how long I'd been working on it, surely I should have been able to master that by now?

'Well, Victoire, are you going to make up your mind?' It was their wedding anniversary dinner, we were all dolled up for the occasion, Dad had chosen a great restaurant and now here was I pissing them all off with my little crisis, like some poor little anorexic, because I wasn't even capable of making an effort to please them. Mum and Léo were staring at their (empty) plates and Alex was going pale.

I realised I wasn't going to get out of this one.

The waiter arrived and I asked him if it would be possible just to have a plate of steamed vegetables. Dad rolled his eyes to the heavens, but said nothing, and the others ordered. When the vegetables came, it was immediately obvious they were swimming in oil. 'They're not "swimming in oil", Victoire. They've just been dressed with a drop of very good olive oil. This is a gourmet restaurant and they feel obliged to do that.' Maybe they did feel obliged, but there was no way I could eat that. In four days' time, I'd be arriving in New York and I had to be able to get into the clothes. You'd have thought he didn't understand, or refused to understand. He raised his voice. Alex was as white as a sheet, Mum had tears in her eyes and Léo looked completely lost. I started crying. Between sobs, I apologised and explained that I couldn't help it, but that I'd eat a full plate of vegetables, promise, so long as there wasn't any oil on them.

Dad gave in and, because he was angry, he asked the waiter in a very curt tone to take away my plate and bring me another one without any oil or sauce. I stopped crying and we finished the meal in a deathly silence. I had brilliantly contrived to ruin their wedding anniversary.

When I'd finished my huge plate of food, I went to the toilets to try to make myself vomit. I knew that it was really dangerous for my health, but this was an emergency situation and I had no other choice. But I couldn't manage it and only the following day did I find the solution; I wondered why I hadn't thought of it sooner. Mum always carried laxatives and various medicines in her toilet bag, 'just in case'. If I took enough of them just before meals, the food I ingested wouldn't have time to stay in my system and release the calories it contained, meaning that I would at least be able to get through the final days of the trip without having to go through the restaurant scene again. I would agree to eat a bit more to reassure them and I'd take laxatives on the sly to eliminate it all.

I went and stocked up at the drugstore while they were tanning themselves on the beach. I had what I needed and nobody was any the wiser. But why hadn't I thought of it sooner?

I was also hoping that the laxatives would soothe my stomach aches, but you can't have everything. Laxatives couldn't do much about the anxiety that was gripping my guts, but if they at least enabled us to spend our last three days here as a family in relative tranquillity, that would improve things no end. I could see that Dad was happy to see me eating vegetables and chicken and I was very happy to see him happy. I adore Dad. It wasn't his fault if he didn't understand.

And then I bought myself a suitcase! A supermodel's suitcase: not too big or too small, all black and shiny, and adorned with flowery straps so that I could pick it out easily at airports. And Mum got me a pretty, bright pink Filofax in which I'd be able to note down all my appointments. So now I was operational.

Alex loaded up my iPod with tracks by Coldplay, Lenny Kravitz, Robbie Williams, Curry and Coco, Pony Pony Run Run, Renaud Capuçon, Eric Clapton, Lilicub, Téléphone and Simon and Garfunkel so that I could be with them all the while I was away: I just had to put on my headphones to hear what my brother had playing in his ears and wanted me to have playing in mine.

On the morning of 30 August I snapped my suitcase shut and Alexis took it down to the hotel lobby. I resprayed Yùki with Mum's perfume and slipped him into my bag. I swallowed a quarter of the tranquilliser she had given me, and which had already helped a lot when I'd taken the plane on my own three weeks earlier.

I went down to join them. The taxi arrived, and that's when I began to cry. We all got into the cab and I said, 'I don't want to go. I'm not going to be able to manage it.' Léo started to cry.

Dad said, 'You're worried now, because you don't know what's in store for you and these last few weeks have dragged on. But soon enough you'll see, Sweetpea: in the heat of the action, you'll be fine.'

Mum added, 'He's right, Loutch. In less than three weeks, you'll be home again. And you'll see, between now and then it will all go by very quickly.' But there was a catch in her voice and then she began to cry too. Alex, for his part, said nothing.

We arrived at the airport and they all came with me to departures. I was still crying, Mum too, and even Léo, who was giving me little kisses on the hand. Dad's eyes were dry, but strangely bright. Alexis came and hugged me very tightly in his arms and said, 'Sis, you're the most beautiful girl. And I love you.' He had tears in his eyes – and he never has tears in his eyes. And he never says things like that.

I embraced them all one last time and then off I went. Right then, I felt as if I no longer existed at all.

New York

I TOOK ANOTHER QUARTER of the pill in the plane and felt like I was in the process of dying of grief. And of anxiety. I thought of Mum constantly, wondering how I was going to keep going for seventeen days without her. Seventeen days, when I was missing her so much after just two hours! I went and had a cry in the toilets and tried to calm myself down by taking deep breaths. I splashed my red eyes with some water so that I wouldn't look like a drowned rat when I arrived at JFK. Back in my seat, I hugged Yùki against me and tried to get some sleep. My mind was a swirl of images. Alex's anger, Léo's kisses, the Grand Canyon and Venice Beach, the scenes with Dad and his worried look, the way he called me Sweetpea and Mum called me Loutch, the walking exercises by the pool, Beverly Hills and Marilyn Monroe's grave in Westwood Memorial Park in Los Angeles, Granddaddy's hands trembling and him saying, 'my little Victorinette, you're driving me up the wall,' and Flo's voice merging with that other nasty little voice, which was becoming more and more insistent. And then the adorable little affectionate messages that they'd slipped into my Filofax, unbeknown to me.

Mum's tears …

Seb was waiting for me at the airport, just the same as ever: an enthusiastic and over-the-top windbag. I felt bizarrely pleased to see him and all the 'my darling, we're going to take them by storm' stuff even comforted me a bit. We headed off towards the Chelsea neighbourhood of Manhattan in a big chauffeur-driven car. Seb took a large folder out of his bag. It contained a telephone with my New York number, the keys to 221 West 16th Street, apartment 3C, where I would be staying with Olympe and Madeleine for three weeks ('They arrived last week, they can't wait to see you again'), a map of New York on which he'd marked one cross showing the apartment and another showing the location of Silent ('You'll see, it's just up the road, ten minutes on foot') and the list of all the people at the agency I'd be dealing with, their phone numbers and also the contact details for the French embassy ('Just to be on the safe side, but you won't need them. After all, I'll be with you almost all the time'). I very much hope not, Seb, because you're already starting to wear me out!

He dropped me off outside the building and said, 'Get to bed early. Tomorrow I'll come and pick you up at 8.30.'

This really was New York, with its brownstones and the black steel fire escapes on the façades, just like in the films! I lugged my case up to the third floor and used my key to open the door after I'd rung and got no reply. The girls were lounging on the sofa in the living room, watching TV. They vaguely murmured hello. Yes, clearly delighted to see me again! I had no idea why, but it was obvious that they were in a sulk with me. In the end, they did rouse themselves to show me round the apartment: I had the bigger bedroom, dominated by an enormous bed that seemed to beckon me into its embrace. In the kitchen the cupboards were desperately bare: a packet of tea, a tin of coffee, a bit of fruit and some 0 per cent yoghurt in the fridge. 'I suppose you haven't brought any provisions? You can have one or two of my fruits tomorrow morning. We go to the market at the end of the day, and you can buy stuff for yourself there.' Why, Madeleine, thank you for your kind offer. The bathroom was a mess and there was a second bedroom at the end of the corridor, which they were sharing. How lucky I was to have my own room! I thanked them and went straight into my bedroom to text Mum. She wouldn't be able to answer, because they would still be on the plane, but she'd get it when she got to Roissy.

I emptied my suitcase, filled the room with my things so that I would feel at home and put my scales at the foot of my king-size bed. My first New York weigh-in read: 47.1. Well done, the laxatives. I was really proud of myself: I'm going to get into the clothes, Flo, I'm telling you! I sent another text to Mum to share the good news, put on my night T-shirt, swallowed a sleeping pill to make sure I would be on form tomorrow and nestled up to Yùki, who smelled almost as nice as darling Mum. It was 32°C outside, but I was feeling pretty cold as usual. So much the better – I'd never have got to sleep otherwise in such humidity.

Mum's call woke me: she was at the airport, they'd just arrived and were waiting for their luggage. It was good to hear her voice. I described the apartment to her and told her about my schedule for the day: this morning, Seb was picking us up to take us to Silent and this afternoon it would be the first castings. Dad had been right: the prospect of working was making things easier and, above all, I was feeling less anxious. I was just in a hurry to get going!

I was about to hang up when Mum said in a worried voice, 'I got your second text, Loutch: 47 kilos is really too little for your height. Promise me that you'll never, ever go any lower than that.'

'I promise, Mum. I won't go any lower.' Except if they asked me to, naturally. I would see what Silent had to say in a little while.

Seb kept us waiting for at least forty-five minutes. Apparently, it was like that every day. It really got on my nerves – I can't stand waiting. That greatly amused Olympe and Madeleine: 'Poor thing, it's not looking good for you, then. Being a model is all about spending your life waiting! But we'll let you find that out for yourself.' They were sniggering at me and looking at me in a funny way. I didn't know what I'd done to deserve it, but it was making me feel uncomfortable. And it made me sad too, just like it had at secondary school before I left, when I found myself alone and the other girls ignored me disdainfully. I didn't give a damn, I didn't give a damn, I didn't give a damn. I wasn't there for them, I was there to become *the* top model of fashion week and I couldn't wait for it to start at last.

When Seb eventually turned up without offering a word of apology, the four of us hit the streets of New York to make our way to the agency. The heat was overwhelming, but I was rapt with wonder. We crossed through the massive Chelsea Market, where you can find absolutely everything you could wish to eat and where I would be able to stock up on fruit and fresh vegetables. To my eyes, everything was new and beautiful and wonderful. For the first time in weeks, I was genuinely happy!

On the way, Seb explained once again the principles of the castings: every morning, we would stop in at the agency to get the daily schedule they had planned for me. They were up to speed on all the castings of the day and would choose the ones I should attend, depending on the status of the designer and his specific requirements, if any – for example, some only accepted blondes (I'm a brunette) or girls over 6 foot or very thin girls – and also depending on whether they had managed to speak to the designers directly about me or not.

'And so I'll have appointments at set times?'

Olympe and Madeleine sniggered at me again.

'Yes, when you're Claudia Schiffer, honey. Then you won't even need to go to the castings, or you'll jump the queue ahead of everybody else, because you don't make Claudia Schiffer wait. But until that happens, you queue up with the others. If you're lucky, you'll get called quickly. If not, you'll wait for ages – and nice and patiently, without complaining.'

I could sense that my days were going to be long.

Silent's offices were located on a very chic Chelsea avenue lined with upmarket boutiques. But to go inside, you had to locate a tiny door hidden away in the corner of a cul-de-sac. This opened onto a small corridor that had been freshly painted white, as had the narrow staircase that led up to a landing, where there was a row of letterboxes opposite a large lift. The place smelled of paint, as if they had still been decorating up until the day before. The agency was on the second floor. Behind an unremarkable door, there was a huge loft space that was also painted completely white and which seemed to dwarf the team's office area. It was very attractive, but also very empty and extremely quiet. We were a long way from Elite's Parisian beehive. Breathing in the vapours of fresh paint, I wondered how long Louis and Émile had been based here. They projected the image of top professionals, but could it be that they were every bit as inexperienced as I was and just as full of big talk as Seb? Everybody knew Elite, but Silent?

But it was a bit late to be asking such questions now. They greeted me warmly and enthusiastically, just like the last time we had met. Mathilde, Louis's wife, was there too – a gentle and smiling presence. And also the adorable Quentin, a huge New Yorker who was very 'oh my darling', like all the people here. He was the one who handed me my schedule for the day: that morning, my first casting was with Alexander Wang and there were four others to follow in the afternoon. He was almost apologetic that things were starting so slowly for me, but promised that things would be picking up in the coming days. I very much hoped so, because that was what I was there for.

Picking up on the murderous stares from Olympe and Madeleine, Seb decided that he would take all three of us there together by cab: 'We're going to stick together. You're going to this morning's casting on your own – he only wants ultra-thin girls. We'll wait for you in the car. But you'll all be doing the afternoon ones.' I could understand why they were sulking: for a start, that sly little allusion to their weight (they'd lost weight since Paris, but not as much as I had) and then the fact that they would have to wait for me, as if they were at my service. That was hardly going to improve relations between us.

The casting was in a very attractive former factory in SoHo, located in a quiet street. The concertina gates of the gigantic goods lift creaked as I shut them and then opened them again on the seventeenth floor, which was a huge space of brickwork and riveted girders. Through the large bay windows, the view over Manhattan was breathtaking. I really felt like I was on a film set. There were no other aspiring candidates in view. The place was completely deserted, apart from a small office in front of a window and a young woman sitting at a desk. Very thin and dressed entirely in black, she greeted me with a booming voice and a big smile: 'Hi! What's your name?'

I advanced towards her on my 7-inch stilts. The uneven white floor was a maze of traps with all its holes and slits. If I wasn't careful, I was going to fall flat on my face. I introduced myself to her and put my book down in front of her.

'Where do you come from? Paris! OOOOhhhh! Paris! Can you walk for me please?'

I turned away from her and started my parade, doing my best to follow all the procedures: relaxed shoulders, supple pelvis, no Playmobil hands … At the end of the line, I turned around and walked towards her with determination, staring at a point in the distance as Évelyne had taught me to do and trying not to be caught out by that damn floor.

'OK. Once more, faster and stronger?'

And off I went again. I sped up and took large strides as if I were in a hurry, turned around and bore down on her, silently cursing the bloody floor. She took a comp card, closed my book and handed it to me with a rather curt 'thank you'. And it was all over.

It was a very useful two-point lesson: first, I absolutely had to find myself another pair of shoes. These ones took too long to put on, they weren't stable enough and my feet must have slimmed down too, because I didn't feel well enough supported in my stately Balmains. Second, I had to learn how to walk more quickly. My tempo had evidently irritated her: too slow and too staccato.

Seb agreed with me (for once!). We dropped the increasingly furious girls off at the subway – they would go to the afternoon castings without us – while we headed directly to

Aldo on Fifth Avenue to find some shoes: 5½ inches of heel minimum, and maximum comfort. Fortunately we weren't talking the same prices as at Balmain, because this time I was paying! I hunted out two pretty pairs, one beige and one black, which were elegant and comfortable and endorsed by Seb: $150 for the two. And then we went back to the agency, where I spent two hours walking around in my new acquisitions, listening to Quentin's advice on how to walk at pace while remaining alluring. I now understood that everything moves faster in New York – I had to get with the rhythm of the Big Apple, and fast.

By the end of the day, I was exhausted. And despite the stifling heat that pervaded the city, I felt cold. I hadn't eaten anything since my morning Pink Lady, but I wasn't worried about that. I just wanted to go home, take a shower and call Mum from my bed to recount my chaotic first steps. We'd been texting each other all day long, but I really needed to hear her voice.

But I was out of luck – Silent had invited us all out to a restaurant to celebrate our debuts! We just about had time to stop off at Chelsea Market to buy some fruit and then at the apartment to change. And then it was back in a cab and off to a packed and noisy restaurant full of people like us: this was clearly the big gathering of fashion week. We went over to the bar and everybody ordered white wine except for me – I went for Diet Coke. And then we waited and waited and waited. My nasty little voice kept on wondering how I would manage not to eat in this restaurant. 'If you eat, you'll get fat

and you won't be able to get into the clothes any more.'
Putting on an ounce on the very first day was unthinkable. I
couldn't understand why Louis, Émile, Mathilde and Seb,
who expected us to be as thin as rakes, hadn't thought of
that. They spent their whole time ticking off Madeleine and
Olympe for being too fat, and then they invited us to a
restaurant!

By eleven o'clock, we still hadn't been seated and so I
decided to go off to bed. I apologised to Louis, who couldn't
believe it: 'You're so professional, Victoire. Good on you! Get
back safely.'

And so I got a cab. It was too late, or too early, to call
Mum. I felt both happy and sad, enthusiastic and discour-
aged, and disgusted and starving. I ate a little piece of honeydew melon which I'd bought at the market – it was a delight.
So I cut off another piece, and then another, and then another.
Soon, the whole melon was gone. What an idiot I was – no
willpower at all. Before going to bed, I took three laxatives in
the hope that they would compensate for my weakness.
Before lying down, I weighed myself: I was finally bang on
47. Phew! But I wouldn't feel completely at ease until I was
given some clothes to put on. And I managed to get into
them.

Casting Hell

I QUICKLY GOT INTO THE RHYTHM: get up, shower and have a piece of fruit while waiting for Seb, who was invariably late. When I asked him why we didn't just meet at the agency, he replied, 'Listen, Victoire, you're not going to start doing your star act, are you? Go with the flow, that's all you're being asked to do.' Olympe and Madeleine were delighted to hear him snapping at me. Things weren't going smoothly between us. The reality was that I was doing three times more castings than they were and it wasn't working out very well for them. You had to be blind not to see why: it was all very well them being slim and pretty, but they were distinctly more fleshy than most of the very thin girls in the queue at the castings. And the reason was simple: even if they ate light food, and not very much of it, they ate, and drank, a lot more than those of us who were on an extremely strict diet.

Apart from a few rare exceptions, who seemed to be able to eat three light meals a day and never put on an ounce (and even then, I'd have liked to see what they were doing when they locked themselves in the toilets and what substances they had in their bags), we were all on the same diet: chewing gum and Coca-Cola Light to stave off the hunger and boredom, with a piece of fruit or a 0 per cent yoghurt from time to time.

It didn't bother me unduly. Mostly, I didn't have time to feel hungry. The scales were always hovering around 47 and as soon as they looked like going up a bit, or when I'd nursed my evening blues with too many melons or nectarines, laxatives would fix the problem. They were very effective, though I did have to up the doses. It seems that the body adjusts quickly ...

I fully understood what was expected of me: I had to be a young woman who was fresh-faced and pretty, never moody and with no needs or desires of my own except to conform to the desires of those who were selecting me. And, above all, never stressed-out. Designers had the monopoly on stress: they were the ones whose career was on the line at the next fashion show, who were exposing themselves to rave reviews or devastating criticism and who were taking all the risks. All we had to do was be good 'clothes hangers', as Karl Lagerfeld put it. Slim, efficient, a winning walk and a killer gaze. Next please!

I'd also understood that when you were a model, eating in public was simply not the done thing. You absolutely had to give the impression that you weren't interested in food, or indeed in anything at all except for fashion. Which suited me – I stopped carting around books, or even magazines, in my spacious bag, because I just couldn't concentrate on a chapter, an article or even so much as a paragraph. It was as if my brain couldn't digest anything any more except for Alex's music, which was on a loop in my earphones. The ideal thing was to have the completely detached air of a girl who wasn't interested in anything, least of all the other girls, or else only to make fun of them, as the Russian girls did. They always stuck together and seemed to spend their time trying to undermine the competition, looking us up and down, giggling and passing comments, all in a language we couldn't understand.

Seb even had a go at me when the other girls told him that I was 'too nice' at the castings and that I engaged in 'conversations' with models from other agencies. 'Be careful what you say to them, Victoire. The others don't need to know what's going on in your life. We're your family, not them.' But of course you are …

Fortunately, in the midst of this horde of rivals who were all a bit on edge (and it has to be said that the pace was frenetic – I was doing between twelve and eighteen castings a day, so I was very careful that nobody jumped the queue in front of me), you did meet a few nice girls who it was pleasant to spend some time with while you were waiting for your turn. To start with, there was Ludmilla and Tania, the two other girls from Silent, who were a bit older and more experienced and who were always very considerate and maternal towards me. I would have loved to share an apartment with them.

And then I met Kate, an adorable Canadian who was always pleased to bump into me so that we could speak a bit of French amid this sea of Anglophones. Pauline, who was a very sweet Belgian, walked me through the whole complex history and politics of her country. Céleste, a sublime and very sweet-natured blonde from Holland, dreamed like me of one day becoming an actress. We were the same age and had a similar background. A lot of models are between 14 and 16 years old and it's not often you meet slightly more mature girls with an education whose ambitions extend beyond being selected for a fashion show or an ad campaign! Céleste and I quickly became friends. She'd been on the circuit for a year and already had the impression that she'd seen everything this little world had to offer. And she hated it. When she confessed to me that the hardest thing for her was the loneliness, I felt less lonely. It was a very strange feeling – I spent my time surrounded by loads of people, always ready with a 'my darling' or a 'honey' or a 'sweetie', and yet I had never felt so isolated.

I used to shiver with cold and loneliness from morning to night, despite the crowds and the New York heatwave. It was so hard, and I don't know how I managed to stick it out. I'd cry in bed every night. Fortunately Mum was there at the other end of the line.

She would console me, encourage me and give me the strength to hold on for that little bit longer. Sometimes I felt like going home. She persuaded me to stay, at least until I found out if I was going to be chosen for a few shows. 'After all, that's why you're there. Castings are a pain and they're dull, but if they choose you for a show, it'll be fantastic!'

Louis had warned me that they always made up their minds at the last moment. We were informed the day before, two days at most – it was unpredictable. 'But if it works out, you'll see – it's like a fireworks show!'

In the meantime, I scurried from casting to casting, criss-crossing New York without ever seeing anything beyond what I could glimpse through a cab window. When I could, I walked. It was good for my figure and I could get some fresh air. Thankfully, we'd had time to look around a bit as a family and so I knew a few of the landmarks and I also had some happy memories.

Something horrible happened to Céleste. She had suffered so much from being alone during her first year as a model that she had got herself a really cute little dog that she used to travel with – her very own Yùki, except hers was alive! But at the beginning of the week, he got sick and nearly died. She had to miss almost a whole day of castings, including one very important one, to take him to a vet clinic for treatment. And it cost her an arm and a leg into the bargain. She later found out that the two Russians from her agency who she was sharing an apartment with – 'You know, the type of girls who are capable of tripping you up and making you fall down the stairs so that they can get your job?' – had been stuffing her dog with sweets so that he'd fall sick and she'd miss that really important casting. They were out of their minds! This profession was full of nutcases! Céleste got her revenge as best she could: she got hold of the two girls' make-up brushes and patiently rubbed them in the dog litter. Two days later, their faces were covered with spots – the score was even …

Even though my relationship with Olympe and Madeleine wasn't getting any better, we fortunately hadn't reached that point yet. They really weren't nice towards me, but, deep down, I sort of understood them. My model pupil side must have irritated them, but I couldn't help it. Whatever my scales might have said, I lacked lightness. I was so scared of not doing things right that it made me anxious. And one of my ways of dealing with that anxiety was to do the best I could, the absolute best, which made me come across as a goody-two-shoes. I could see that it exasperated them. They might have realised that it wasn't directed at them, if only Seb hadn't kept on comparing us: 'Look at Victoire – she's not eating, is she? Look at Victoire – she goes to bed early, doesn't she? Look at Victoire – she …' If I'd been in their shoes, I couldn't have stood it either!

Things reached a climax the day he found some sweets hidden in the kitchen. He used to regularly rummage through their stuff to check that they weren't eating anything they weren't supposed to, as if he were their father and they were 12 years old. And he made a right scene: 'How do you think you're going to succeed if you eat all the time? And then you're surprised when you don't get booked for any shows! Even at the castings, they're not interested in you any more. What's the point in being here if you just get rejected everywhere you go?' I felt so sorry for the poor things.

The next day I found myself alone with Seb between two appointments and he took me to a salad bar for lunch. He loaded up a huge plate and devoured it all in front of me while I nibbled at three spinach leaves and a mini-portion of chicken without sauce, pushing the croutons and parmesan shavings to the edge of the plate. 'You're a genuine pro, Victoire. That's what I try to make the girls understand, but the message won't sink in.' I seized the opportunity to ask him to stop making these comparisons all the time because it was making my relationship with them difficult. Naturally, that very evening he decided it would be a good idea to have a go at them for that as well. The guy was a real jerk.

Hallelujah, I can get into the clothes! Some of the designers would get us to try on a few of their designs during the castings. The first time that happened to me (it was a pair of silky trousers), the little voice inside my head was screaming, 'You're too fat, you're not going to get into them. If you carry on eating, you won't be able to get into them.' I got into them, and with ease, even. If you wanted to be sure of things fitting, 47 kilos was the right weight. So long as I didn't put any weight back on, I'd be fine.

Apparently, I was going down well and Louis and Émile were delighted; they told me they'd had some excellent feedback, that more and more directors were calling to invite me to castings and that I was definitely going to be chosen for loads of shows. I hoped they were right and that I wasn't putting myself through all this for nothing.

Castings are very tough. There we were like a herd of cattle, trussed up in our skinny jeans and tops, perched on our high heels and waiting our turn to be judged from head to toe in sweltering heat. Generally, you went on in the order that you arrived. There was an itinerary every morning and Quentin would indicate in red which appointments I had to prioritise. I tried to be among the first to arrive to cut down on the waiting time as much as possible, but it didn't always work out like that. The casting director, the all-powerful god, was the one who decided how things proceeded. Sometimes we would wait for hours on account of shambolic organisation or because the big chief wanted to revel in his power.

One day, I waited for an eternity in a very strange space of about 300 square metres, which was rather dilapidated and completely empty. There was a red carpet that ran from the entrance and crossed the whole apartment as far as a very large room down at the end, where it turned at a right angle and passed in front of some completely overexcited guy who spent the whole time yelling, 'Yeah! OK! Walk, walk! I love you, baaaabyyy!' At the entrance, a woman was taking the books and the comp cards and getting us under starter's orders: 'Your turn! Go!' Off I went, walking at the New York pace beneath the light from the huge projectors and a barrage of shutter-clicking, courtesy of the three photographers present. The closer I got to the yelling guy down at the end, the more agitated he got. I don't know what drug he was on or what mental illness he was suffering from, but it was frankly scary. I came out of there feeling like you do after seeing a horror film – completely dazed!

On another occasion, I had to resist the urge to retch when a very thin designer came over to adjust the pins on the outfit he'd asked me to try on. He smelled as dirty as he looked. He was clearly also on something pretty strong – he was constantly running his fingers through his hair and vigorously scratching his scalp, dislodging clouds of dandruff which then settled on his black shirt. He spent ages yanking the cloth of my dress every which way, and I really thought I was going to vomit.

But first prize for really taking the piss undoubtedly went to the casting directors at Calvin Klein, Nikki and Ashley, who were peerless champions of the art. They were like grotesque Laurel and Hardys, kitted out in clothes of no discernible gender (dresses, turbans, make-up) and totally absorbed in their little routine, which involved playing the hysterical lovestruck clowns. They would pick us out in groups of five with a wag of the finger, without taking any notice of the order we'd arrived in. 'You, you, you, you and you. Oh, not you.' And then they sent us into a small room where our outfits were waiting for us on heavily laden racks. 'This one for you, that one for you.' As if they were playing with dolls! I ended up with a very pretty little black dress which I was in the process of slipping on when the girl next to me asked me to swap. On her hanger there was a light, rather see-through dress. 'I'm wearing a black thong, and that's all they'll see!' I pointed out that they'd chosen this black dress for me and that it probably wasn't a good idea to switch. 'OK, do you mind if we swap thongs, then?' I beg your pardon? How could this girl not know that light underwear was compulsory in this profession? I refused to swap my thong with her. She thought I was being horrible. What I found horrible was the idea of wearing somebody else's knickers.

We were their playthings – docile, submissive and consenting toys, who were theirs to do with as they wished. And none of us even dreamt of protesting. Once this circus number was over, they gave us back our books.

I think that was the day when I consoled a tall pale girl with beautiful, very long red hair who had started to tremble before bursting into tears and muttering, 'I'm not going to make it. I don't know how to walk. I'm not going to make it.'

I could so understand why she was cracking up! I reassured her as best I could by passing on some of Évelyne's tips – relaxed shoulders, supple pelvis, watch the Playmobil arms – but above all by repeating to her Peter's precious words, which had done me so much good when we'd had dinner at his place in Beverly Hills: 'If you don't treat the whole thing as a game, it's going to kill you.'

She looked at me as if I were a Martian and then she couldn't stop thanking me for having been 'so kind' and for having taken the time to comfort and reassure her.

'Don't mention it, it's only normal!'

'It might be normal, but in this world of nuts, people are so inhuman that you sort of forget what normal is.'

And then, just once in a while in this vast free-for-all, you caught a glimpse of a shooting star – a really pretty girl who exudes something different, something both light and powerful. Something scintillating and self-evident. She turned up as if in a hurry, her hair, make-up and outfit all impeccable.

Freed from the obligation of wearing the standard skinny black trousers, she had turned up at the casting in a pretty and very sexy pair of shorts and an attractive top to match. There wasn't a hair or a blemish on her stunning well-oiled legs. Not a blotch on her fair skin, not a fault in her taste. A kind of luxuriant perfection. The casting director came to greet her in person and in French, with an accent you could cut with a knife. 'Constance! I'm so pleased you could make yourself available! Please come in. And how are you doing, my darling?'

Her name was Constance Jablonski, *the* top French model of the moment, the winner of the Elite competition in 2006 and the muse of Estée Lauder and, much more importantly, of Victoria's Secret. She was a year older than me and already had a glittering career under her belt. Exactly what I was hoping would happen to me.

Russell Marsh

THE CLOSER THE FASHION SHOWS approached, the crazier everybody seemed to get. I was feeling increasingly stressed and tired out. I couldn't understand how Olympe and Madeleine, who I would hear getting home at two nearly every morning, managed to keep going. I didn't go out at all. The previous week Émile had invited us all over for some food at his rooftop apartment in one of the chicest parts of SoHo. Well, invited us so to speak, because in fact we all turned up with our own little salad boxes, purchased at the deli next to where he lived. But it was actually quite practical that way, because we could watch what we were eating and not be tempted to veer from our diets.

I was the first to arrive and I was really stunned when he opened the door. I don't know if it was by managing models that he'd earned enough to buy an apartment like that, but the place was dazzling: a large, very bright living room that gave out onto a huge teak terrace with a sublime view over the whole of Manhattan. 'Take a seat while I have a shower.' And as he said that, he started to get undressed right in front of me in the middle of the living room. For a moment, I felt extremely uncomfortable and I just had time to notice that he had impressive pecs underneath his crumpled linen shirt before I fled out onto the terrace, keeping my back to him and hoping that the others wouldn't be long in arriving.

Nothing happened, of course. Émile was no doubt amused at my discomfiture and I couldn't help remembering how embarrassed I'd been when I'd arrived at Sergei's seedy studio in Paris a few weeks earlier; that seemed all such a long time ago. I didn't know this world, but the glimpse I'd had into it so far had confirmed that I'd been right to keep my distance from such a peculiar environment, where all sorts of creatures and predators prowled and substances abounded. I felt like a little girl catapulted into a world of adults. And so, when two hours later everyone had finished their aperitif (Pepsi Max for me) and Ludmilla announced that we were off to a party at Quentin's – 'I hope you've brought your swimsuit, Victoire? Wait till you see the incredible apartment he's got, with a swimming pool on the roof. The parties there are just crazy ...' – I declined the invitation. I wasn't armed for these 'crazy parties' on the rooftops of New York. But more than that, I didn't feel like it. I was feeling cold and exhausted and I wanted to go home and call Mum.

I was missing her terribly. The two of us were counting the days until I was back in Paris. The time seemed to be dragging interminably. We texted each other all day long and then spent ages on the phone every evening between me going to bed and the sleeping pill kicking in. The aches and pains – in my legs, in my stomach and above all on my skin – were getting worse. When I went to bed in the evening, it felt like my entire back was cracking up, as if I were a snake shedding its skin.

Fortunately, though, in the course of this mad helter-skelter, I also had a few extraordinary experiences and encounters. I was lucky enough to be spotted by Russell Marsh, one of the most powerful casting directors in the business. Every year at the start of the season, he chose two or three new faces who he would take under his wing and transform into elite models. I was one of his choices and so, at his request, I attended the castings of all the designers he worked with. And there were plenty of them! It was a pleasure, and even an honour, to be picked out from the huge crowd of all the other models and I started to believe that perhaps Seb hadn't completely over-rated my chances of having a genuine career as an elite model.

At each of his castings, Russell Marsh greeted me by my first name in his perfect British accent and with an encouraging smile. He seemed to really trust and believe in me – he introduced me with a great deal of affection to the designers as the 'little nugget of the year'. In the midst of all this American excess, his Old Europe side, his London elegance, his bright eyes and the special attention he paid to me were like a rallying point and a source of comfort. He really could have been a member of my 'family'.

He had so much faith in me that he asked me along to the Ralph Lauren casting, despite the fact that the designer only ever chose blondes. It was a very unusual experience. Sitting behind a large desk, Ralph Lauren welcomed us with his wife, his two sons and his daughter at his side – an elegant array of beautiful, blue-eyed people. I'd naturally put on the little dress that I'd bought in Vegas and which I'd been wearing virtually constantly since I'd been in New York. I washed it every evening and it would dry overnight, ready for use again the next day.

'Hello, young lady. What's your name?' His eyes were extraordinarily blue, but also very kind. It was pretty rare to be greeted with such consideration, particularly by such a big name in fashion.

'Hello, my name is Victoire, and I'm from Paris.'

'That's great. And you have a very pretty dress! I'd never have thought of wearing it like that, but it works really well.'

I smiled, walked around for him a bit and smiled once again.

He took one of my comp cards and handed me back my book: 'Thank you once again for coming. Have a nice day, young lady.'

I know it's silly, because nothing amazing happened, but I couldn't get over it. It was scarcely believable to find myself being treated so kindly.

There was also a huge casting organised by Russell for three or four designers simultaneously – there must have been more than 300 hopefuls – at which we were each given a little black cloth bag with a few goodies inside: a coconut water drink, a notepad and pen, a 'Fashion Week S/S NY' tank top and a compilation CD featuring the hits of the summer. It was nothing fabulous, but in the middle of this massive cattle market we were taking part in unpaid in the hope that it might get us a bit of work in the coming weeks, and in the middle of all these castings where we'd stand around or sit on the floor and wait for hours and where most people would bark 'next!' at us by way of greeting (sometimes accompanied by a snap of the fingers) without even deigning to look at us or smile, even the most minuscule mark of consideration felt like a genuine gift. We were all delighted!

One morning I had my first and only unisex casting, and it was for Lacoste! After days on end spent in the company of other girls, I was really pleased to be around some boys, a lot of whom were French. In the middle of the group, I immediately spotted a blond guy with green eyes who was even more handsome than the others: he was absolutely gorgeous! We didn't speak to each other – it wasn't the time or the place – but I thought to myself that it would be cool to be chosen to parade with him.

And then one afternoon there was this timeless moment in a very attractive suite in a top hotel on Upper East Side, all of whose windows looked out onto Central Park. The designer had set up folding screens and clothes racks in the adjoining rooms, which gave the place the feel of one of Marie-Antoinette's very elegant antechambers. As I waited my turn, I admired the beautiful late afternoon light filtering through the trees and looked forward to the long walk that I was going to treat myself to in Central Park once the casting, which was the last of the day, was over. But again I was out of luck: Quentin called me to give me another appointment and off I went, promising myself I'd return here as soon as I could.

But of course I never got the opportunity, because we spent the whole time running around left, right and centre. Running around without eating a thing. And waiting, hour upon hour upon hour.

One evening at around ten o'clock, a few days before the first fashion shows, I had just finished talking to Mum and had turned out the light, when Quentin called: 'Victoire, I've got a casting for you! But it's right now. Where are you?' I told him I was in bed, that I'd taken a sleeping pill and that I didn't think it was a great idea for me to get out of bed under the circumstances. 'Are you kidding? It's Samuel Drira, a great French designer, and he's called on behalf of Russell Marsh. If he likes you, he'll take you for the shows for the three brands he's overseeing! You can't afford to miss this.'

I got up, got dressed and jumped in a cab, struggling against the relentless effects of the sleeping pill. I found myself in the small entrance hall of a smart private residence, furnished with pretty pink and red round chairs.

Everything around me was floating. I went down a long corridor, at the end of which a man was waiting for me. I vaguely remember seeing some racks full of clothes and apologising for being a bit sleepy. He replied very sweetly that he was aware that it was very late. I suppose he must have got me to try on one or two designs and to walk for him, but I have no memory of it at all. I've no idea what happened afterwards, or who put me into a cab, or who helped me to get upstairs and into bed. The following morning when I woke up, I was incapable of piecing together the end of the evening.

Between two castings, I was chosen by Narcisso Rodriguez's team for a fitting, which meant for a start that I found out what a fitting was, and above all it meant that I got to know Louise. She was also a model and also French, and I had time to have a good chat with her. The two of us had to act as living models for the designer, who adjusted his designs directly on our bodies while referring to his drawings. Initially, I was pleased to be part of a design session and it was certainly more interesting than parading endlessly in front of casting directors with their unpredictable moods. And on top of that, it was paid work! But I lost my enthusiasm a bit when I realised that I was in the presence of a designer who was super-stressed-out about his upcoming show and that I would have to endure all his mood swings and all the pricks of his clumsy needles. Louise was positively furious: Narcisso Rodriguez had been using her for his fittings for four years, but never for his shows. She also worked for Elite and had won the competition in 2005. Since then, she'd been living in New York with her man, but her whole family was from La Baule, where she had grown up. It was so nice to be able to have a long conversation about that part of the world.

When she realised that I was here with Seb, her reaction was vehement: 'Ditch that loser as soon as you can! He's a liar and a bullshitter. For four years now he's been telling me that he's turning thirty! I bet he told you that you were the new Claudia Schiffer and that you'd have the world at your feet?'

I couldn't really bring myself to admit that to her, because I felt rather stupid for having believed him at times when he'd said that.

'Maybe it's true, Victoire. The fashion world is pure roulette. But after four years, I can tell you that most of the girls are working really very hard for nothing much in return. You reckon that when you sign a handsome contract with a big agency, then you've hit the jackpot? That's not the case at all. Of course there's plenty of money involved, but most of it goes to the agency and to reimbursing your expenses. In the end, you're left with barely 10 per cent of the amount stated on your contract.' She was categorical: the only way of genuinely making money in this profession was to be chosen as the muse of a major brand. 'But how many contracts are there like that in the course of a year? And have you seen how many of us there are in the market?' She'd been lucky enough – she was really very beautiful – to have been chosen by Chanel and Ralph Lauren. 'That's meant that I can live well and buy myself an apartment in New York. But not much more than that.'

A life like that would do me just fine! Perhaps it would even allow me to get myself known and slowly get a career in theatre or film off the ground?

I expressed my surprise that she was here doing castings and fittings when she'd already been Chanel's muse. 'After the competition, I worked like mad and really watched myself. And then after three years, because it was all going well, I took my foot off the pedal a bit and put on 5 kilos. Instant punishment! I was no longer of interest to anyone! I've slimmed down and am making a comeback, but I've got to start all over again from the bottom. This business is a war zone, Victoire. There's no quarter given.'

So I'd have to wage my war, then. I was really proud of myself for not putting on an ounce since I'd been in New York and I was hoping that my efforts would bear fruit. At the end of these trying ten days, I was on my way to one final casting with Seb and the girls – I don't remember which avenue we were on exactly. All of a sudden, on a crosswalk, the skyscrapers started to spin around me. I lost my balance without understanding what was happening to me. I heard Seb call out my name, I said to myself, 'That's it, it's all over,' and then everything went blank. When I came to, I was lying on the pavement, the girls were giving me something to drink and Seb was coming out of a salad bar, where he'd got me a small piece of chicken. I realised that I had fainted in the middle of the street, out of fatigue and for lack of food. Seb suggested calling a cab so that I could go back to the apartment and rest, but I refused. After the chicken, I was already feeling better.

When we arrived at the casting, a very sweet young woman gave each of us a form to fill in: height, measurements, weight. It was the first time since I'd been there that somebody had asked me how much I weighed. Very proudly, I wrote down 47. The girls were around the 60 mark. We handed in our forms and, a few moments later, the designer came to fetch us. Or to fetch them, anyway, to try on the designs. He didn't take me. 'I'm sorry, Victoire. You're gorgeous, but you're really too thin: 47 kilos just won't work! My clothes will be hopeless on you.' I went down to join Seb in the taxi and wait for the girls. I was pleased for them: for once the tide had turned in their favour, and it was about time.

But it didn't save them from having to pack their bags a few days later. Silent had let them know that it wasn't worth them staying: they weren't going to be selected for any shows. I felt truly sorry for them, and I think they believed me. They suggested we went out to dinner together the night before they left and naturally I said yes. I was so hungry for a dose of humanity and so in need of the slightest sign of affection! We spent a really pleasant night together, them tucking into a New York feast and me with three steamed vegetables in front of me. They didn't say sorry for having been so unfriendly towards me, but I sensed that they no longer held anything against me and that they understood that I wasn't to blame for how things had turned out for them.

As we were ordering, Madeleine said to me very kindly, 'Victoire, you can't live like this! Eating so little is no kind of life.' I replied that the shows were starting in two days' time and that I had to be certain of getting into the clothes. 'But you can get into the clothes, Victoire! Can't you see how thin you are? Look how you fainted because you hadn't eaten anything!' I smiled at them but said nothing. I didn't want to offend them.

Maybe I was thin, but earlier that day Louis had called to tell me that I'd been chosen for at least three shows and that there would no doubt be plenty more. And here they were, going back to France empty-handed …

Three, Two, One, Go!

WE COULD HEAR THE MURMUR of the crowd on the other side of the wall. We were made up, coiffured and manicured and already in our clothes and shoes, all ready to go. And we were excited. The tension mounted by the minute, and then by the second. I had arrived three hours earlier with Seb, who for once wasn't late. If he had been, I reckon I'd have killed him, or at least ditched him for good. The warehouse where the show was being held was opposite the agency and so I hadn't needed his help getting there. But, all the same, it was good to have him with me.

I'd tried the clothes on two days earlier and hadn't had any trouble getting into them. Jen Kao, the Japanese designer, liked flowing silks and airy fabrics. For my first catwalk, she'd assigned me a strappy dress which was very soft and had a very low neckline, with off-white lace and trimmings. And for the second, a large indigo-blue lace top which was very transparent and through which you could clearly make out my breasts, or what was left of them. This went with a very short white skirt and a shirt with an attached silk scarf printed with large blue and white flowers. My hair was swept back, as if

I'd just come out of the sea, and my eyes were heavily outlined with dark black make-up. And like a gift from heaven, I also had little white ultra-flat sandals made of white lace! There was no danger I'd be breaking my neck on account of high heels. We'd been shown the catwalk a little earlier: it was a large triangle covered with sand and the public were sitting in the middle of it and around the edges. My first catwalk was going to have the look of a walk on the beach.

Everything had been made ready for me: my name was displayed on the canvas chair placed in front of a mirror surrounded by bulbs, and a make-up artist, hairstylist and manicurist were waiting for me. All I had to do was put on the dressing gown draped over the back of the chair and sit down. Then they set about me, initially one by one and then all at the same time, preparing me from head to toe. I let them get on with it, observing their every movement. I asked them to explain what they were doing, because I wanted to learn more about and understand these new professions, which were now a part of my own profession too. The make-up artist told me what colours I should choose to bring out my eyes. The hairstylist gave me something to help my hair stay in good shape throughout fashion week. The manicurist quietly went about transforming my fingernails and toenails into little iridescent seashells. I was one of twelve models, all of us lined up in front of twelve mirrors and each with a little team busying itself around us. Photographers were also flitting among us with their lenses trained. There was a growing buzz of activity and excitement.

The next stage was getting dressed. My outfits were waiting on hangers bearing my name and with Polaroids attached to them which had been taken two days earlier. All I had to do was put on the dress and sandals and put the scarf round my neck and I was ready. But even that I didn't do on my own: there was a dresser there to help me. I was more than a little embarrassed when she got down on her knees to lace up my sandals. I apologised and she looked at me with big round eyes, saying with a laugh that it was the first time a model had treated her with such consideration! Her name was Joy and she was a student. She worked as a dresser during the fashion weeks to earn a bit of extra money. I confessed that I wasn't used to having somebody at my beck and call like this.

'Relax! Don't feel as if I'm at your service, but rather that we're both at the service of Jen Kao. My job is to make sure you don't stain the dress with your make-up, mess up your hair when you put it on, or crease it by bending down or trying to put on your shoes.' Put that way, it had a certain logic about it. 'And you'll see, you'll be very glad to have me around during the show to help you change your outfit in two minutes flat in a little while, before your second catwalk.' I thanked her and explained that this was my first fashion show. She wished me good luck with a friendly wink.

And now there I was with the others, behind the wall. We were under starter's orders. Jen Kao, who came to inspect us discreetly, was visibly tense. We all tried to reassure her as best we could by telling her how much we liked her clothes, how happy we were to wear them and how we were sure that 'they' were going to love them. Personally, I wasn't sure of anything any more, other than that we were experiencing something exceptional. And that even if it was all completely artificial, it felt really good to be sharing these emotions.

At the beginning of the corridor that led to the catwalk, a woman all in black, got up like a warrior in her combat boots, baggy trousers, T-shirt, walkie-talkie and earpiece, was holding firmly on to the wrist of the girl who was due to open the show. On the other side of the wall, the chatter gradually subsided. I felt a little nerve begin to twitch in my upper lip. Stay calm, Victoire! Focus! There was an almost religious silence and then the music suddenly boomed out, like a starting gun. 'Three, two, one, go!' The first girl was pushed out into the light on the other side of the wall. My heart was beating faster and faster. Second girl.

It was about to be my turn. Third. The woman grabbed my wrist firmly, and my chest was pounding. 'Three, two, one, go!' I felt the sand under my feet and the projectors blinded my eyes. I knew the public was there, all around me, but I couldn't see them. Staying focused, I advanced in rhythm towards the point of the triangle. It felt great! I was filled with an amazing energy, which I could feel all around me and which was exploding in my legs, my stomach and my brain. Shoulders, arms, large strides, looking straight ahead. Going forward into the middle of the flashbulbs, overcome with this phenomenal strength welling up inside me.

I felt infinitely light, as if I were flying.

When I got backstage, there was only one thing on my mind: to do it over and over again! I wanted to go back out and get that unbelievable, dazzling jolt of lightning again! Joy helped me to change in silence. I had to stay focused. Retain the energy that was filling this warehouse with its magic waves. And here I was next to the warrior again. 'Three, two, one, go!' Yes, I'm off! It was so good, so intense, so wonderful. Louis had been right: it was a fireworks display, and I was one of the rockets!

But it lasted barely a moment, and then it was over. We all gathered again behind the wall, excited and relieved at the same time. Jen Kao joined us for one last parade all together, and we were greeted with applause. I felt so full of joy. I was happy to be there, I loved this world, I loved fashion and I loved the whole planet.

I loved my life full stop!

I wanted it to be brimming over with moments like this one, which was like nothing else I'd ever experienced before. Wow! It was incredible, magical and unique!

Joy was waiting for me backstage to take back the clothes, but the make-up artists and hairstylists had already disappeared from their posts. We all got dressed again, laughing with excitement. Seb appeared and laid it on with a trowel as usual. 'My darling, you were ab-so-lutely fabulous! Sublime! Ex-tra-ordinary!' I let him roll out his spiel while I savoured the moment for myself. Louis had just texted me: 'Well done, Victoire! We watched you on the internet and you performed like a queen! We're waiting for you.'

We crossed the street back over to the agency and when I opened the door, Louis, Émile, Mathilde and Quentin got up to applaud me. It gave me shivers of excitement and pleasure. That evening, all alone in my deserted apartment (I never thought I'd miss the girls!), I called Mum and described everything down to the very last detail. I was exhausted and both happy and sad, excited and depressed. I told her the day would have been just perfect if she could have been there to experience it with me.

The Heart of Fashion Week

WHEN I WOKE UP the day after my first show, I found a lot of sweet words and affectionate messages of love on my computer. Back home, they'd been able to watch me on the internet while I was sleeping. Granddaddy and Nan wrote to say that they were proud of me. Alex and Léo said that I'd been the most beautiful girl. Mum and Dad said that I'd been right to stick with it and that the whole thing was great. All that did me the world of good and I told myself that perhaps my beautiful life as a model was finally beginning.

But I didn't really have much time to think about it: the days that followed were one long whirlwind. Louis was right: the requests to do shows started to flood in. 'This is great, Victoire. You probably don't realise it, but a novice never gets as many bookings as this!'

Everything unfolded at a crazy pace. The following day, after a show for Doo.Ri, the Korean designer, I had the pleasant surprise of receiving a lovely present: the assistant opened a room full of clothes and accessories from previous collections and invited each of us to choose $500 worth of merchandise! I thought that was very sweet, even though I was a bit frustrated: I didn't really like anything I saw and everything was absolutely tiny. Even weighing 47 kilos, I wasn't sure I'd be able to slip into the clothes. But I did find a pretty, very dainty black linen cardigan as a present for Mum and a very figure-hugging dress for me, which I'd only be able to wear if I didn't put on an ounce. Which was ideal, because that was my objective: to remain at 47 kilos, because that's what seemed to appeal to them.

Today was a madhouse! I had three shows in the afternoon. For Trías, a Spanish designer who makes very precisely structured clothes, I experienced the strange sensation of walking on a podium with my legs at the public's eye level. And also the pleasure of doing my first interview, in English, in the wings just before going on stage! The journalist doubtless chose me after seeing that I spent the whole time talking to everybody else: I was filled with wonder at it all and genuinely interested in everything that was happening around me. Unlike the other models, who kept mainly silent with their headphones permanently clamped on and their eyes glued to their telephones, I chatted to the make-up artists, the hairstylists and the dressers with real enthusiasm. I so much needed and wanted human contact!

Next up after Trías was Custo Barcelona, which involved loads of extensions in my hair, off-the-wall multicoloured geometric dresses and completely hysterical music. It was odd to say the least, but we certainly had fun!

And then I hurried along to DKNY, the Donna Karan ready-to-wear brand, which was a must at New York fashion week. The outer garment was no problem – I slipped into a perfect night-blue trench coat, which was tightly belted up – but the shoes were a real nightmare! Gorgeous, original, sexy and completely unwearable. They were prototypes made out of a very hard material and were thoroughly uncomfortable, attached to the ankle by just a large ribbon and featuring Himalayan heels. How were you supposed to walk in such things? I felt the panic welling up as my feet turned into two little points of unbearable pain. I walked up and down in the wings trying to get used to them and to get my balance, before deciding that the best solution was to sit down and spare my poor feet until I had to go out onto the catwalk. What sacrilege! One doesn't sit down when wearing catwalk clothes. My bottom had barely touched the seat before an assistant was telling me to get up again.

I set out on the catwalk trying not to think of the bloomers they were always showing on TV to entertain people, where you see the ankles of poor models buckling and them falling over to a chorus of belly laughs. The decor was a bit unusual, in that we had to negotiate our way through large coloured cubes on which the spectators were sitting. And so there I was walking among the guests without the protection of the darkness in which they usually sat, or the shield of the blinding light that normally prevented us from ever seeing them properly. The main thing was not to catch anybody's eyes, otherwise I was bound to fall over. So I set my gaze on a distant point and tacked gracefully among them, hoping that I would make it safely back to port.

Everything went fine until the finale, when we all went out in single file to take the applause. I don't know how the others managed it, but I just couldn't keep up with them! I could see the distance growing between me and the girl in front of me and I felt ridiculous. I was sure I was going to get a dressing-down, but in the end nothing happened.

During those short moments of euphoria that always followed a show, when the tension dissipated and we congratulated each other on a successful event, nobody came up to me to suggest that I should learn how to walk. I took off my torture shoes with huge relief and a wonderful sensation of freedom.

As usual at the end of a show, a scrum of photographers was waiting for us. They were shouting, 'Jacquelyn, Jacquelyn, smile please!' and seemed to be addressing themselves to me. I stopped and smiled at them and was about to tell them that my name wasn't Jacquelyn, when Jacquelyn Jablonski, a blue-eyed brunette like me and one of the media darlings of the moment, appeared. She shot me an icy look, struck three poses and then disappeared. And then they asked me, 'What's your name, honey?' I told them, and they all repeated in unison, 'Victoire! Victoire!' And so I happily posed for them, while wondering if, with a certain inevitability, I'd just made my first enemy in the profession.

The next day I did a show for an English designer. Having got my make-up and hair done well in advance, I had the time to have a proper conversation with an adorable Russian model, who told me that this profession was her only means of escaping from the poverty of her family background. She explained that this was why most of the Russian girls were so competitive and aggressive: they had no choice, because this was their only hope of avoiding a desperate future, of getting a taste of luxury, however fleetingly, and of travelling around the world. We were in the middle of discussing all this when an assistant came to tell everyone that the TV people were here. I saw all the models head for the buffet – there was nearly always a buffet backstage, normally consisting exclusively of forbidden foods, except for some fruit – and start tucking into the cakes and the muffins, which did look particularly appetising, it's true.

I couldn't believe my eyes: how could they allow themselves such an indulgence right in the middle of the fashion show period, whereas I was constantly being harassed by that bastard little voice, which would force me to make amends for the tiniest bit of chicken breast with a whole pack of laxatives? The answer came soon enough. As soon as the TV crews had moved on, the girls rushed off to the toilets, obviously to make themselves vomit. Everyone knew what was going on, nobody spoke about it and life resumed as before, as if all this were normal.

The show must go on.

There was quite a surprise at the end of the show. I heard the photographers shouting, 'Victoire! Victoire, a smile

My very first 'pola': lips open, chin down,
concentrating on my look.

At my first meeting at Elite agency in Paris.
I've just put pen to paper.

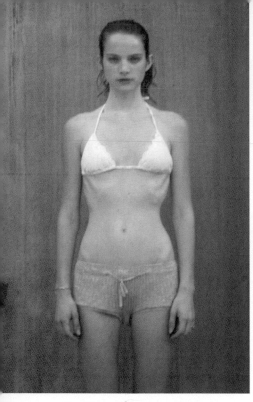

Too big to fit a size zero. I eat
three apples a day to match the
measurements on my comp card.

No sun for me. Designers want us
as white as a blank canvas.

Back to polaroids for the castings. I'm improving my look, it's starting to kill.
Casting directors take pictures from all angles. Skinny jeans, white or black and
body-tight, high heels and no make-up. No smile. Nothing more.

Arrived in my flat in Chelsea, New York. I'm 47 kilos at 5' 10", finally the right weight to be a real model.

My new life: 18 castings a day, running through NYC with my heels and a book in my bag.

Backstage at the shows we spend most of our time waiting. Make-up artists, hair stylists, dressers and assistants recreate everything on and around you.

And before it's beautiful, it's often painful.

Sitting in DKNY clothes, before the show started (strictly forbidden!). Photographers are invited backstage to take style pictures. It was impossible to stand in these shoes, even Donna Karan said it herself.

Doo.Ri show in NYC. Thanks to this picture, people online call me the Catwalk Yeti.

Complete change of style for Custo Barcelona, still in New York. Very loud music calls for a big, flamboyant walk.

Paris. At the end of the show we can risk a smile.

With Australian designer Colette Dinnigan at the closing of her show in Hôtel Maurice.

I now own the prized killer look of the Alexander McQueen show at the Musée de l'Homme in Paris. My brother Alexis is among the photographers.

Photographers waiting for us models at the end of the Vanessa Bruno show in Palais de Chaillot, Paris.

Waiting, waiting, waiting for the Miu Miu campaign in London.

Photoshoot for Lacoste. Even a size zero is too big for me now. I am disappearing.

Back to life in Regent's Park, London. Studying, smiling, following my dreams.

please!' I may have made myself an enemy the day before, but clearly I was known by my first name now.

At Silent, they were delighted: it seemed that people on the scene were beginning to talk about me and that 'everybody' had noticed the little French girl who was on the rise. According to Louis, whose pronouncements struck me as more reliable than Seb's (I really couldn't bear his superlatives any more), it wasn't beyond the bounds of possibility that the brands would soon be fighting each other to have me in their campaigns. I could only hope he was right! This profession was only appealing when things happened quickly, when things sparkled, when things crackled! That was what I wanted – that, or nothing.

For the time being, I didn't know how much I was earning from it all, but I knew how much it was costing me. The better the news was for the agency, the worse it was for me. Because although I would of course be returning to Paris, it would be for one night only. The very next day, I would have to head off to castings in Milan, where I'd be holed up for nearly ten days, and then it would be back to Paris for October fashion week. I didn't want to do it – I needed to rest, spend time with my parents and brothers, finally see Sophie again to tell her the whole story and go to the cinema with my cousin Thomas. I needed to spend an afternoon with Nan and with Granddaddy, whose health was deteriorating, to stroke my little Plume and to hug my darling mum …

* * *

I was having more and more trouble sleeping. I constantly had the very painful sensation that the skin on my back was going to crack up. When I went to bed, I could feel every one of my bones and just couldn't find a comfortable position. And then there was my stomach, which was a constant source of suffering. High doses of laxatives were no longer enough to set my mind at ease. The moment I ate something, even if it was just a piece of steamed fish or a quarter of a honeydew melon, I felt as if I were swelling up like a balloon. And yet I'd seen the photos of my first shows and the film we'd made between two castings for Silent in the garden of a photographer's house in Brooklyn. In them, I was thin, diaphanous and ethereal. And I liked what I saw – I preferred people to see my bones rather than my fat!

A slightly embarrassed Mathilde pointed out a little detail that greatly embarrassed me: in the photos of the Doo.Ri show, all my body hair was standing to attention! I had a clear memory of shivering in that room, where the air conditioning had been much too strong and I'd had goose pimples. 'You have to shave yourself, Victoire. Your arms and your thighs.' I agreed with her about the thighs: I'd never realised I was so hairy! Although, actually, I suspected that I wasn't really that hairy and that it was probably the cold, the backlighting and the super-powerful camera lenses that had created that impression. But my arms? I wasn't about to shave my arms! On the phone that night, Mum agreed that it was a very bad idea. If I started shaving my arms, I'd have to carry on shaving them for the rest of my life! It was out of the question.

I had another show for the very minimalist Matthew Ames, for which I wore some very beautiful pleated and draped fabrics. And then another for the exuberant Dennis Basso, who designs dresses for princesses with wonderful furs. I went to try them on a few days beforehand in his studio in the middle of the Bronx. I turned up in a huge chauffeur-driven Hummer ordered by the agency. I felt like I was travelling in an armoured vehicle! It was at this show, as I changed from a sublime silk mesh dress with white mink into an amazingly elegant black sheath dress with a neckline edged with fox fur, that I met a young model who was barely 16 and who was with her mother. It was possible, then? Perhaps Mum could come with me to Milan! I absolutely had to talk to her about it, and to Seb. I reckoned it was the only way I'd be able to carry on in this profession and feel genuinely happy. At least for the time being.

I rounded off my fashion week in style with Phillip Lim's show. He was an absolutely adorable designer, and I loved his style. There was a sort of professional love at first sight between us. I immediately took to his chic, modern and inventive clothes and to his refined and discreet trademark look. But above all, I liked his sunny kindness, his gentleness and his thoughtfulness. When I went to try on the clothes, I was greeted with the same surprise as at the Doo.Ri show: a treasure room full of previous collections, and the girls in the show could choose $1,000 worth of freebies! I helped myself to two wonderful dresses, which I'd probably never wear

because they were so original, a large pair of denim dunga-
rees and a very attractive black leather and suede bag with a
very refined finish, which from now on would never leave my
side.

Phillip was the only one of the New York designers who
had chosen to present his collection in a real-life setting, as
they often did in Paris: we paraded at the American Museum
of Natural History, and it was sumptuous! The outfits were
magnificent and the atmosphere was in keeping with the
man: gentle and elegant. The one source of anxiety for all the
models was the prospect of slipping in our beautiful platform
clogs on the mirror-polished parquet floor. A few minutes
before we got under way, I saw him all alone in the corner,
nervously biting his nails. Seeing him like that touched me so
much that I went over to him and gave him my opinion: his
collection was sublime, at any rate I loved it, and I was certain
that all of 'them' would like it too. He seemed so taken aback
that I wondered if I'd spoken out of turn, but then he thanked
me warmly. I think that little dose of humanity, sincerity and
kindness, exchanged between us in the midst of all the excess
and the pervasive cynicism, did us both good.

There was another surprise waiting for me at the end of
the show. In addition to the photographers calling out my
name as I left, suddenly a bunch of rather shy but excited
girls appeared and asked me to pose with them, wanting to
know all about the clothes I was wearing. Slightly confused,
I told them that I was wearing a little Ralph Lauren dress
from the children's collection (which really made them laugh)

and Aldo shoes and that my beautiful bag was designed by Phillip Lim. All this seemed to fascinate them.

In the cab back to the apartment, Seb, who had witnessed the whole scene, explained that I'd just been spotted by the female bloggers who assiduously followed all the events and gossip of fashion week. 'This is great news, Victoire. It means that you're starting to be identified as the rising top model. I told you, sweetheart – we're going to go down a storm!'

But for now, all I wanted to do was pack up my bags and go home. One last show was scheduled for the following morning with the Canadian Jeremy Laing, and then I'd be on my way to JFK airport. I packed that evening so that I would just have to pick up the cases after the show and jump straight into a cab.

I must have caught a chill, picked up some bug or eaten something I shouldn't have done (though God knows, I only ate fruit), because I was sick all night. Or perhaps it was my body telling me to put an end to this exhausting diet of incessant stress and pressure. When Seb came to pick me up for the show, I was in the toilet throwing my guts up. He said we could cancel; models did sometimes fall sick, in which case they were urgently replaced. But I refused categorically. I wasn't about to finish my New York fashion week with a cancellation! I took the appropriate medicine, drank a large glass of Pepsi Max and off we went to Jeremy Laing. I could hardly stand on my own two feet, but I knew I'd pull it off. Either you're a pro, or you're not.

Home Sweet Home

I SPENT THE FLIGHT snuggled up in the big white sweater that Dad had bought me from Abercrombie when we arrived in New York. I caught my reflection in a mirror at the airport and I realised that I really did have the perfect figure for clothes like these, which I would never have dared to wear six months earlier. Big white sweaters are only pretty on thin girls. Fortunately it also had a fleece lining, because I was shivering even more than usual, no doubt on account of exhaustion but also because of the emotion of going home, even if it would only be for a few hours.

And I'd had to fight even to get that: Seb had been planning for me to fly directly to Milan from New York. I thought I was going to kill him there and then, but instead I said that if it was going to be like that, then I was quitting completely. Initially, he didn't believe me, but he eventually realised that I was serious and, miracle of miracles, what had been 'absolutely impossible, darling, it's much too complicated' suddenly became entirely possible. I needed to remember that for future occasions.

Mum and Dad were waiting for me at the airport when I arrived. How glad I was to see them again and how lucky I was to have such wonderful parents. The boys were there when we got home. I really did love them. I unpacked my bags and gave each of them a little present, which I think they were pleased with. Alex made fun of my curly hair, which was a result of Jeremy Laing giving us all African braids. He also showed me the search results when you googled my name – it was crazy! I saw the photos of the shows once again but, above all, I discovered what people had been saying about me. 'Wait till you see the best comment of all,' Alex said, and showed me a post where somebody had said that I looked like a man and called me the 'yeti of the catwalks' because of that photo where I had goose bumps and you could see my body hair. And there was another one from a girl who I didn't know at all saying that she knew me and that I'd 'always been a bitch'. All this made Alexis crack up, but what he didn't realise was that, for me, it was hurtful. I made up my mind never to google my name and I asked them never to tell me what was being written about me.

My little Léo gave me a thousand hugs and Plume nestled his face up against my nose, with his paws on my neck, and spent the night purring. It felt so good to be home and I didn't want to leave again.

I didn't want to go to Milan. It was too much effort, it was too soon and I wanted to give up this profession.

* * *

Mum packed my suitcase, because I was crying too much to do it. She promised that she'd do her best to join me out there and reminded me that it would only be for a few days. On top of that, there was no time difference with Italy and so we'd be able to call each other much more easily. 'It's the 18th today, my love. It's just one week. On the 25th, you'll be back here for Paris fashion week. And then I'll be with you all the time and it'll be great, you'll see. We'll be able to do everything together.'

And so off I went to Milan. My spirits were low and my guts were in a mess, and I hated myself for my inability to decide what I wanted in life and to stick with the plan.

I travelled with Louis; Seb was already out there waiting for us. I liked Louis a lot and he was very sweet towards me. We talked quite a lot in the plane and he told me how he'd fallen in love with this world and this profession, but that he could tell that the same couldn't yet be said of me. He shared his vision of things with me: he'd wanted to create an agency on a human scale, where quality was more important than quantity. He liked to take care of the girls he worked with and to bring out the excellence in them rather than sending them anywhere and everywhere. And he understood that for 'girls like you', it was difficult to adapt. 'I realise that, most of the time, you're with people who aren't particularly interesting and who don't have much to say for themselves. But I assure you it's worth persevering. For a start, because you're very talented and things could work out really well for you, so it's a great opportunity. And also because if you learn to manage your career properly, you could lead a very exciting existence, earn lots of money and do what you dream of doing in life.'

I didn't dare tell him that I really wasn't sure what kind of life I dreamed of any more. What I wanted to be was an actress, but I wasn't at all sure if the path I was on was going to lead me there one day.

There's that incredibly moving scene in Andrzej Zulawski's *That Most Important Thing: Love*. Romy Schneider plays a completely desperate actress who has to immerse herself in a stupid role that she detests. She says to the director, 'I just can't do that,' and the director screams at her, 'You're under contract, you're paid to do it. So do as you're told.' A photographer is snapping her and she suddenly turns towards him and says, 'Don't take any photos, please. I'm an actress, you know, and I can do good work. What I'm doing here is just to put food on the table, that's all. So please don't take any photos.' I think I understood better than ever at that moment what she meant.

It was raining in Milan and Seb was waiting for me at the airport. He was totally different to Louis, who I said goodbye to with some regret. Now it was back to the endless stream of banalities uttered by 'my' agent. Louise was right: if I carried on in this profession, I'd have to do it without him. It was just all too unbearable. I was introduced to Riccardo, the student who would be my chauffeur for the whole week ('So much more practical than a cab!') and to his little hatchback, a Renault Clio, which really wasn't ideal for my long legs. I had to fold myself in two, and even four, just to get into the back seat. Naturally it didn't occur to Seb for a second to offer me the front seat.

Our hotel was quite a long way out from the city centre, but it was pretty. I immediately started wondering where I was going to be able to do my shopping and get hold of my fruit in this far-flung suburb. There was a big bouquet of flowers waiting for me in my room with a little message from D' Management, my Italian agency, welcoming me to Milan. It was very kind, but I was none too sure that it would be enough to ensure that my week there would be a pleasant one.

Milan

THOSE EIGHT DAYS IN MILAN were so awful that I wish
I could forget all about them. Despite the warm welcome
from the whole team at D' Management, who I met the day
after I arrived, things kept on getting worse.

My initial fears were borne out: I couldn't find anything
suitable to eat close to the hotel. On the first evening, I
ordered a platter of fruit and they brought me three
sorry-looking apples which battled for space with a bunch of
grapes, all for an exorbitant price. My little voice immediately raised its tone: 'You're going to get fat. Nobody's going
to choose you. Paris fashion week is screwed.' Panic took
over, and although I thankfully had a good stock of laxatives
with me, I knew I should never have come here. The week
was getting off to a very bad start.

First up, there was the Gucci casting, which took place in
a sinister-looking old building where Riccardo dropped me
off in the pouring rain. The clouds were so low that it felt
almost like night-time in the middle of the day. I found myself
waiting in a dark corridor among a group of completely silent
and motionless girls, who looked half-dead as they stood in

a line in their 7-inch heels. There was absolutely nowhere to sit down, and flopping onto the floor like in New York was out of the question. They were all good little obedient soldiers, standing to attention and simply waiting there for somebody to deign to call them.

When it came to my turn, the casting director beckoned me over without a word. I said hello and introduced myself, but she didn't reply, and neither did the two lackeys at her side. With another gesture, which was very close to a snap of the fingers, she indicated that she wanted me to walk. I complied and executed a little round trip. Then she gave me back my book, from which she'd taken a comp card, and I left the premises, feeling a strong urge to turn around and find the courage to scream at them that we weren't cattle and that they might bring themselves to treat us like fellow human beings.

I took it all out on Seb in the car and, for the very first time, he raised his voice with me: 'Calm down this instant, Victoire.' I screamed that I wasn't going to calm down, that I hated this crappy city and that it was completely unacceptable to be treated like that. 'You're just going to have to deal with it, aren't you? Who do you think you are? You're just a model. You do as you're told and you keep your mouth shut.'

Right! I'd made up my mind: I was leaving this city, I was ditching this loser and I was quitting this profession.

I packed my bags to return to Paris and called Mum in tears to tell her that I'd really had enough this time and that I was bailing out. She listened to me, consoled me and calmed me down. And then she said the magic words: 'Don't leave, Loutch. I'm on my way.'

She needed a day or two to organise herself, but the prospect of her joining me instilled a bit of courage in me. The next day I dropped in at the agency and Francesca, who was the assistant to the bookers and really adorable, showed me something that really pepped me up: a website devoted to models called the Fashion Spot had opened a fan page for me! I couldn't believe my eyes! I skimmed through the very sweet and complimentary comments and wasted no time in sending the link to Alex to prove to him that not everybody thought I was a 'hairy bitch'!

Chatting with Francesca, I also realised that their relationship with Seb wasn't all that good either. I said I was surprised to have had so few castings – four or five a day, in contrast to the twelve to eighteen appointments I'd had every day in New York. Slightly embarrassed, she hinted that he was the one who was opposed to them sending me to all the places where I could have gone. This made no sense to me at all. 'We don't understand either, and seemingly Flo at Elite in Paris, who I've had on the phone a couple of times, is in the dark too.' I realised that I'd need to get an explanation out of that imbecile soon, but I wasn't sure that I had the strength to confront him.

I was still feeling really furious with him when Riccardo came to get me for my hair and make-up session at Prada, which my dear Russell Marsh (who wasn't in Milan but who was continuing to look out for me from afar) absolutely wanted me to take part in. He'd contacted the very powerful and respected Miuccia Prada, who ran the great design house founded by her grandfather with an iron rod, to let her know that I was here. When Riccardo heard me slagging off Seb, he looked at me with a big smile and then came clean: he couldn't stand having Seb on his back any more either. Always late, not exactly friendly, arrogant, pretentious, completely vague in his instructions and with a shaky command of the English language. '*Vittoria, non so come sopportarlo!*' I don't speak Italian, but I didn't need to look in the little dictionary that I had purchased to understand: Riccardo and I were very much in agreement on the subject!

And now here I was, booked from midday until three o'clock for a make-up and coiffure session at Prada without even having had to go to the casting. I wasn't sure if the omens were good: I remembered how Louise had been chosen for all Narcisso Rodriguez's fittings without ever being selected for his fashion shows. And she'd warned me: 'The hair and make-up sessions are even worse. They massacre your skin and hair with all their experiments, and then they go and choose perfectly fresh girls for the big day!' But Francesca had calmed my fears: 'On the contrary, if Signora Prada wants to see you, then that's a very good sign.'

I was pleasantly surprised to see Pauline there, the Belgian model who I'd got on quite well with in New York, and also that very young American who'd been over there with her mother. We waited for quite a long while – in Italy, time-keeping is often somewhat relaxed – and Pauline had time to tell

me a bit about her experiences: her agency had sent her to
China, where she'd worked non-stop for catalogues, ads and
small fashion shows. 'You learn the basics of the profession,
you earn a reasonable living and living in China is great. But
you get zero exposure. If you want to make it in the west or
internationally, forget it.' Duly noted, Pauline! Given that it
was eleven hours by plane from home, I wouldn't have
dreamed of doing it even if I was paid a fortune!

We were finally called into the studio, where a team of hairstylists and make-up artists was waiting for us. They were so
wrapped up in their conversation, interspersed with gales of
laughter and much hand gesturing, that they didn't deem it
necessary to say hello to us. Generally speaking, the hairstylists and the make-up artists were my best allies: I would chat
with them and get them to recount their adventures in the
business. They were always sweet and considerate, and genuinely surprised that somebody was interested in them. But not
so at Prada. I'd never seen anything like it. They tormented
us for three whole hours without showing us the slightest
consideration: we really were models, or puppets even – dolls
whose hair you could pull and glue extensions to, whose skin
you could smear, brush and rub and whose head you could
raise or lower by pressing on the chin – all to a constant
babble of Italian that we couldn't understand, which was
probably just as well, because none of it was aimed at us.

And then all of a sudden a silence fell. We'd seen an old
lady arrive, who was very diminutive despite her high

platform heels and who had her greyish blonde hair pulled back into an austere ponytail. She neither opened her mouth, nor smiled. Our tormentors were petrified, and so were we. We weren't introduced, but we immediately realised that we were in the presence of Miuccia, the big boss. She came up to me and the make-up artist pulled my arm as a sign to me to get up out of my chair. I looked down to meet Miuccia's gaze, but she wasn't looking at me, by which I mean that when our gazes met, her eyes didn't express any sentiment towards me at all, as if I didn't exist.

She scrutinised me in silence and then the verdict came: she looked down at the ground. The make-up artist apologised, her voice full of anxiety: '*Mi scusi, signora. Farò altrimenti.*' She then jostled me violently back into my chair and all four of them pounced on me, tearing at the skin on my face and pulling my hair out with brushes until I had tears in my eyes; they were erasing three hours' work and trying something different, while Signora Prada inspected the other girls. When she came back to me a few minutes later, I was ready and completely transformed. She scrutinised me once again and gave the barest hint of a smile. Everybody immediately relaxed and Madam deigned to open her mouth. In a beautiful Italian voice like the wonderful Claudia Cardinale's, she issued instructions on fine-tuning my make-up and my pretty triple bun and then disappeared into the adjoining room where the clothes were waiting for us.

They finished off our hair and make-up and then we had to wait for a good hour before each being summoned in turn for the fittings. I spared a thought for Riccardo, who had already been waiting for me for six hours downstairs, and this was surely going to take another three. Seb would be putting in quite an invoice, because he was paid by the hour.

When my turn finally arrived, I made the acquaintance of Olivier Rizzo, a charming Belgian stylist who handed me a pretty dress and chunky, very hard leather Prada trainers in size 5. I asked him if he could find me some size 7s. 'Sorry, Victoire, we haven't got any.' I suggested that I could parade barefoot or in my own shoes, but it was out of the question – Madam wouldn't tolerate me in anything other than her own shoes, no matter how small and ugly they were. And so he helped me get into them, uttering a thousand apologies. Going down two sizes was unbearable and hurt like hell. Olivier consoled me as best he could: 'Be brave! At least if you've got this far, you can be sure that you'll be at the show tomorrow!'

Once again, I waited for my turn while trying to focus on not feeling the pain in my feet. Madam eventually gestured towards Olivier, who took me over to her. Again, she looked at me without seeing me at all and scrutinised me from head to foot in silence. With a gesture, she ordered me to turn around; with another, to walk, and then to come back, and then to advance forward again; and then finally to leave.

I turned to Olivier and said, 'I'm delighted to have met you,' and then I turned away and, trying not to hobble, I went off to get changed. My cheeks and my scalp were on fire and my feet were bleeding. They didn't bother undoing my triple bun, so I left as I was, with the humiliating feeling that I didn't exist at all. Riccardo took me back to the hotel. By the time we got there, it was gone nine.

I hadn't eaten all day and I had no provisions left in my room. Despite the insistence of my little voice, I still hadn't figured out a way not to eat at all, and so I ordered a piece of fish and some steamed vegetables from room service, because I had no other choice. I hated doing it, because their portions were monstrous and, even though I never finished the whole plate, I never restricted myself to the absolute bare minimum. On this kind of diet, I was going to get huge. My scales confirmed it: I was touching on 49 kilos, despite the laxatives.

I took my make-up off as gently as I could. My skin was bright red. And then I set about the bun and something terrible happened: when I combed my hair to try to get out all the glue they'd used to hold it in place, a whole lock of my hair came away in my hand. In a panic, I rang Seb.

'Ah, yes, at Prada they use very aggressive products. Whatever you do, don't comb your hair, or all your hair will fall out! The only way is to run a very hot bath and spend a good two hours in the tub. The product will dissolve and you'll get back your mane of hair.'

I hung up in tears. That bastard had sent me over there without warning me, although he was perfectly aware of the situation. Everybody knew that those products were disgusting, but nobody said anything, because this is what happens in this industry. I felt treated in a way the RSPCA would never allow animals to be treated, and yet everybody kept their mouth shut.

I ran a very hot bath and stayed in it for two hours, plus a good half an hour spent replenishing and drying my hair at a gentle temperature to avoid inflicting any additional trauma on it. It was gone one when I finally got to bed, having remembered to set my alarm for six: if I got chosen for the show, Seb would phone me at around 6.30 and Riccardo would come and pick me up at seven.

But he didn't call – Louise had been right: they preferred fresher girls whose skin and hair they hadn't spent the previous day screwing up.

And, as it happened, I bumped into Louise again the very next day! It was at a casting at a little Venetian-style palazzo, where we were asked to wait in a delightful garden in an inner courtyard. That made a nice change from the dark corridors and austere antechambers. I told her all about my hair and make-up session the previous day and Seb's reaction. 'But Victoire, haven't you got rid of that guy yet? How do you manage to put up with him? Make up your mind once and for all that Elite is your main agency, and good riddance to him.' We were in the middle of laying into him when we saw a very tall blonde Russian arrive, accompanied by two guys in vests with rippling muscles and tattoos. Their skin was oiled and they were covered in gold jewellery. Louise commented in a low voice: 'You see, it could have been a lot worse for you!' We both laughed. I hadn't seen that in New York, but here you often came across these pretty girls from the east, escorted by distinctly dodgy-looking Goliaths, who would turn up in these enormous gleaming cars. It all reeked of coke and dirty money …

When I left the casting, it was pouring with rain. Seb was waiting for me in the car with Riccardo. He got out to let me into the back seat. By the time he'd pulled his seat forward and I'd folded myself into four to get into the back, we were both soaked through. I got cross and had the audacity to ask him if it wouldn't be simpler if he waited for me in the back seat and I sat in the front seat. 'You must be joking, Victoire. I'm a man and I'm not about to sit in the back.' What a wanker.

To top it all off, he announced triumphantly that he'd found a new recruit who was arriving that afternoon: Melissa, a 'very pretty girl' he'd spotted in I don't know what street and who, needless to say, would go down a storm. 'You'll see, she's sublime! A real beauty. I'll introduce you, and I hope you'll get on well.' You can count on that, Seb.

How awful – here was I, thoroughly disgusted with this city, this guy and this profession, starting to feel a stupid pang of jealousy! As if I needed that too. How could I feel jealous about this loser being interested in someone other than me, and to whom he'd doubtless given the same bullshit, rather than feeling supremely indifferent to it all? It was high time that Mum came and got me out of this nightmare.

At the End of My Tether

I MET MELISSA the following day at the first casting, where she joined me with her own chauffeur – fortunately we weren't going to be obliged to do everything together. She adopted a patronising attitude and described how Seb had spotted her, introduced her to Silent and then launched her without further ado into this whirlwind that I knew so well. I felt a little bitter when I learned that, when all was said and done, her trajectory had been a carbon copy of my own, except that she was arrogant, smug and aggressive. And that she was doing virtually all the castings in Milan.

I was devastated.

At the following casting, I was virtually the only non-Russian. I waited for hours amid this hornets' nest of spiteful blondes, who spent their whole time poking fun at anyone who wasn't part of their gang. When my turn finally came and I went over to the casting director, he was in mid-conversation with his assistants, and not one of them so much as looked at me. I put my book on the table in front of them and still they didn't look up. I did a little parade to the backdrop of their clearly very animated conversation and when I got back to the desk, they were still talking. I wondered if I should interrupt them, get their attention and suggest without being aggressive that I could do another circuit. But I didn't have the courage or the energy any more. I took my book from the table and left, convinced that they hadn't seen me and that I'd wasted my time. Seb confirmed this the next day: they'd expressed their surprise to him that I hadn't turned up for the appointment! How rude could you get?

I had one more casting before returning to the hotel, where I hoped there would be an email from Mum announcing that she'd finally arrived. We waited in a grim meeting room, all sitting around a large table and waiting in deathly silence for a door to open and for just a few girls to be let in each time. One hour, then two, three and nearly four. At a certain point, I just couldn't bear it any longer, even with Alexis's music on a loop in my ears. I couldn't get rid of this knot in my stomach, which I'd been carrying around for days from casting to casting, and so I got up to walk around. They all looked at me as if I were committing the deadliest of sins. I just carried on walking up and down, waiting for something to happen in this room, and in my life. I couldn't see how I could spend the rest of my life just waiting for hours on end for somebody to deign to look at me and maybe choose me; waiting for people to treat me like an animal, an object, a clothes hanger; waiting for people to speak to me and use me without knowing who I was; waiting for people to choose me without giving me anything in exchange, except perhaps a bit of money.

I didn't even realise that I had started to cry. Only when I caught the scornful gaze of the other girls and the triumphant smirks of the Russian assassins did I realise that I was in the process of cracking up. I wiped my eyes, and when the door opened to let the next girl in, I just went on in. Nobody protested. They got me to put on a very beautiful long voile dress and I walked for the 'jury', my face stern and the anger welling up inside. I did a little circuit and found myself back in front of the casting director, who asked me to change into another outfit. I said no, one was quite enough. They couldn't believe their ears.

I said goodbye, took my book, got dressed and fled.

I'd been in this profession for a month and a half, and already I couldn't bear it any more. But there was happiness just around the corner: Mum was waiting with Seb in Riccardo's car! I flung myself into her arms, told her that I wanted to quit right that minute, that I didn't want this life any more and that it was just too hard being treated like this. Seb didn't flinch. It was dark by now and Riccardo took us back to the hotel. We went up to my room and Mum listened to me for a long time; she consoled me, comforted me and hugged me. We decided that I'd stick it out until the end of Paris fashion week and then we'd have a serious think about what should happen next. I fell asleep in her arms.

I had the next day off, but Mum and I nevertheless went to the agency to have lunch. Everyone gave her a very warm welcome and said lots of nice things about me, without seeming to be in the least surprised that she was there. Seb arrived with his new bitch and I went out of my way to avoid him. But at one point he said to me in a saccharine voice, 'You're really very tired, my darling. Close to depression, even. You should take advantage of your mother being here to have a bit of a rest.' I caught Mum's expression and I thought she was going to kill him! She couldn't stand the guy any more either, but we'd talked it through the previous evening and it wasn't yet time to send him packing. We'd sort that out with Vladimir and Flo after Paris fashion week.

For the time being, there were no more castings and so I had a free schedule until the next day, when I was booked for two shows, and there would be a third the day after, and then I could go home: the Milan season had clearly been a washout.

It wasn't a conscious decision, but Mum and I simply stopped talking about the whole thing – we both needed a break. For weeks she had been listening to me talk about my anxieties and had been trying to console me, reassure me and give me the strength to carry on. For weeks, I'd been fretting over what was in store for me, how I should go about things, the choices I should make and my ability or otherwise to succeed in this new life that I was confronted with.

Both of us were tired, exhausted even, and so we decided simply to do a bit of tourism. We walked around the Castello Sforzesco, visited the cathedral, from the top of which you can admire the whole city, had a look around La Scala and went window-shopping in the impressive Galleria Vittorio

Emanuele II, with its immense glass-vaulted arcades. On the mosaic floor, we located the bull that brings good luck: legend has it that if you spin round three times on its testicles and make a wish, it will come true. I didn't pass up the chance. My wish was that the Milan bull would turn me into a contented and renowned supermodel – you have to keep hoping ...

We rediscovered some of the Italian friendliness that we'd loved so much during our holidays in Tuscany and which contrasted so sharply with the frostiness I'd encountered since I'd been in Milan. At the hotel that evening, we spent a long time chatting to Dad and the boys on Skype. It was my first family evening in ages! I managed to help Alex with a critical commentary of the kind I used to do at home and which he was having trouble with. He's the scientist and I'm the literary one. After our chat, we turned on the telly and treated ourselves to two episodes of *Desperate Housewives* in Italian. It reminded me a bit of my school years at home with Mum.

The following day, I had an appointment with Stephan Janson, a French designer who had worked with Yves Saint Laurent, Kenzo and Diane von Fürstenberg before creating his own brand in Milan. The show was taking place in his very pretty villa, in the middle of a superb garden. It was billed as a small gathering, but there were some sixty guests all the same. Sporting a large djellaba, he greeted me by my first name, as if I were one of them, from the top of a majestic staircase in the middle of a hall whose walls were covered in mounted butterflies. 'Victoire, I'm so happy you're here! Come out onto the patio, the others are waiting for you!' I was pleased to see Kate was there, the tall red-headed Canadian I'd met in New York. I didn't know the other girls, but the thinness of a small German girl frightened me. How could you let yourself get into such a state? Her complexion was almost green, she had the shining eyes of an invalid and she looked completely exhausted. For a moment, I found myself thinking that she was going to die soon.

Stephan had provided some divans for us to relax on and there was a copious buffet of fresh vegetables and fruit, delicious fruit juices, hot drinks and champagne. He flitted among us, keen to make us feel at home, because he felt that his show would only be a success if we were all enjoying ourselves. 'This is *la dolce vita*, so make the most of it! I've chosen you for your personalities and you're all wonderful. I'm fed up with models who sulk. Have fun, be happy and gay – that's why we're here!'

He was like an angel and I felt as if I'd arrived in paradise. Then it was time to see my outfits: an asymmetrical light cotton dress with a large, off-white strap and another one made of silk and printed with multicoloured flowers, as if to match the butterflies in the hall. And hallelujah, little finely pleated sandals that were completely flat so that we could 'dance, turn and twirl' without any danger of falling over on the catwalk, which was a series of tables set up in the middle of the living room with the guests' chairs around them.

Before the start of the show, Stephan came to see me to tell me that he'd be delighted if I would agree to open and close his show. 'You're like a butterfly, Victoire! When I saw you, I knew that you were made to be an actress. So feel completely free, have fun, be alive and soar!' I was touched, almost over-whelmed, by so much attention and consideration. There was no way he could have known how much his words meant to me and how much good they did me after the dreadful week I'd had in Milan. He served us each a glass of champagne and repeated how honoured he was by our presence, thanking us for having agreed to do his show. This was the world upside down! I drank the champagne and felt the bubbles race directly into my brain and start to fizz there. The music began, he half opened the curtain that separated us from the catwalk and I danced on the tables among the guests with a huge smile on my face. Stephan had made us feel so at home in this wonderful house.

When I came back to get changed, he said, 'That was perfect! Exactly what I had in mind! Thank you, thank you, thank you!' I paraded for a second time to close the show and then went to get him from behind his curtain so that he could take the applause with the rest of us. He was so shy and didn't dare come forward, so I took him by the hand. He was murmuring, 'This is too beautiful, too beautiful,' and he had tears in his eyes.

After the applause had died away and we were back behind the curtain, he took me in his arms and gave me a hug. I hugged him back, this extraordinary man of such refined sensitivity and of such humanity, who had just bestowed on me such an infinitely precious and unique experience.

And then I had to rush off, because that moron Seb had had the bright idea of booking me for another show two hours later, knowing perfectly well that I'd never get there at the allotted time.

It was for Francesco Scognamiglio's collection; he was a wonderful and completely off-the-wall designer, who was already famous for having dressed Madonna and Lady Gaga. I arrived barely twenty minutes before the start of the show, at the same time as the guests. I was sincerely sorry and kept on apologising, but nobody was listening – they just all pounced on me to get me ready. Two manicurists were desperately working on my false nails, which were still colour-coordinated with Stephan's outfits, but they just couldn't get them off. The hairdresser was a magician – he undid my braids and managed to give me a perfect, volume-enhancing blow-dry in a matter of seconds. Meanwhile, the make-up artist was putting on false eyelashes and applying midnight-blue glitter to my eyebrows. At the last minute, I slipped into the sumptuous, shimmering violet-blue satin coat-dress and the towering platform heel sandals with a mauve panther-skin pattern that completed my outfit. I ran to the catwalk and set off just in time, trying to suppress my anger and hide my left hand, on which the manicurist hadn't had time to glue the last three nails.

After the show, I went to see Francesco Scognamiglio to apologise to him. He received me very kindly and said that he'd had a big fright but that fortunately we'd managed to avoid disaster.

Seb was in the car waiting to take me back to the hotel. He said, 'You see, *we* pulled it off.' I chose not to reply and to keep my mouth shut rather than hitting him. I concentrated on what Dad kept telling me: make use of that idiot as the ideal exercise in maintaining your self-control. While coming across as an amateur might not have bothered Seb, I couldn't afford or bear to be amateurish. I was never going to arrive late for a show again and I wanted to have nothing more to do with this guy.

The next day, while they were giving me directions to my last show, the agency sent me the mail that Stephan Janson had written to all the girls in his show, in which he took the trouble to mention each one of us by our first name. He said how 'terrific' we had been and thanked us once again for this 'magnificent' gift we had given him. There was a P.S. addressed specifically to me: 'To Victoire: I'm sure your dad is going to be very proud of you. I can already imagine him seeing you on the catwalks. He really does have an amazing daughter.'

That day's show was taking place in the open air on the Piazza del Duomo. Francesca had managed to find a pass for Mum, who was so happy and emotional about being able to accompany me backstage for the first time and to watch me parade. It might have been a lovely grand finale to a week which even my encounter with the wonderful Stephan hadn't been enough to salvage, but the heavens were against us: like practically every day since I'd been there, it was pouring down and was bitterly cold. The dressing rooms were set up under tents down one side of the square; they were unheated and there was a constant draught. While I was getting ready, I had to argue with the hairstylist so that I could keep on the jumper I was wrapped up in so as to avoid freezing to death. He got his own back by pulling on my hair like crazy.

I wore a very long brownish dress with a very low neckline and peep-toe platform sandals. The hem of the dress soaked up water as it brushed against the wet ground. In the space of two minutes, my feet were soaked. A partially covered corridor led to the catwalk, which was also only partially covered, and the stands where the public, including poor Mum, were sitting, freezing in the rain, were not covered at all. It was a disaster, made worse by the ever-increasing risk that I would get my heels caught in my sodden train and fall flat on my face live on Italian TV, whose cameras were stationed all along the catwalk. Dad had announced enthusiastically that he'd found a way to watch the show live from Paris – well, he'd certainly have something to watch.

All the situation was lacking was a bit of wind, which duly turned up. We started to parade, with Elizabeth Jagger leading the way, in an apocalyptic atmosphere. I could feel my damp dress sticking to my thighs and prayed that it wouldn't wrap itself around my ankles. I did what felt like an endless circuit of the slippery catwalk and then quickly got back to shelter. And only then did I notice that one of my straps had slipped and that I'd been parading with one of my breasts exposed – how delighted my father must have been!

Before we flew back to Paris, we dropped in at the agency to thank them for all their kindness and to say goodbye. Francesca greeted me with her usual warmth and played the show to me: you could very distinctly see my strap fall and my breast pop out, nice and pert in the cold and rain. It made her laugh. 'But it really doesn't matter. You put on a really good show in really extreme conditions. And your gaze was perfect. Wow – what a gaze!' She didn't know me well enough to realise that what she found so 'perfect' about my eyes was massive anger.

In the plane on the way back, Mum showed me the photos she'd taken from the stand: blurred, shaky and wet. 'I was so moved. I was shivering, but I had tears in my eyes. You don't realise, do you? I've got an extraordinary daughter!'

And Now for Paris

MY BED, MY LÉO, my Alex, my Plume, my dad, my mum, my house – I was back home! What sweetness and bliss. Everything was getting better and I was doing better too. Things would improve now, because they were there with me and I would finally be able to sleep at home every night. New York was of course great, but Paris was Paris!

Before the castings got under way at breakneck speed – Flo had warned me by email that my timetable was going to erupt in the coming days – I went over to Avenue Montaigne to visit 'my' agency again at last. I know it sounds stupid, but when I pushed open the door and entered the Elite beehive, which was completely buzzing, it felt like I was coming home. Flo was the first to spot me. 'Oh, Victoire, you're looking gorgeous! Look how much weight she's lost, look how beautiful she is!' They all turned to look at me and started applauding, which made me blush. I felt so proud and happy to be applauded by the Elite team!

Vladimir came over and hugged me: 'Well done in New York, my lovely. You were staggerrring!'

Flo gestured to me to sit down next to her. 'He's right. You had a crazily good season in New York. Now you need to do the same thing here!' She said that as if it were already in the bag and I felt a knot growing in my stomach. She thought I'd lost a lot of weight, but what she didn't know was that the scales that morning had read 49.1. I'd put on 2 kilos in a week. I might not even be able to get into the clothes any more, especially here in Paris. All the girls had told me: here it's size 4, end of story. And for an elite model, Paris is *the* centre of the world, *the* centre of fashion, *the* occasion not to be missed.

Flo said we'd have to sort out the situation with Seb: she had sung my praises everywhere and she really couldn't understand why he'd refused half the castings that I'd been offered in Milan. I replied that for me the situation was sorted and I just wanted to drop the subject. But it wasn't as simple as that, of course; I'd signed a contract and he wouldn't let me go just like that. We agreed to deal with it after the shows because, right now, we had to knuckle down. 'Russell Marsh loves you, he speaks to everyone about you, which is great! He never gets it wrong. You wouldn't believe how many doors he can open for you.' That afternoon I had a casting for Dior and then for Chanel, followed in the coming days by Céline ('Céline is the top of the tree: if they choose you, it's instant glory!'), Balenciaga, Paul & Joe, Miu Miu ('That's a Prada brand, Miuccia will be there', 'Oh please, not Prada! Not Miuccia!'), Ann Demeulemeester, Givenchy, Yohji Yamamoto, Leonard, Valentino, Vanessa

Bruno, Sonia Rykiel, Collette Dinnigan and Alexander McQueen.

I'd planned to head straight to the Dior casting when I left, because they were also in Avenue Montaigne, but Flo warned me that John Galliano was mad about legs. I just had time to go back home, give my legs a close shave and change from my skinny jeans into an ultra-short little dress so that he could admire my pins. Mum took me there in her Mini – she would be my private chauffeur for the day and Dad would take over that evening when he got home from work. It couldn't have been better. We parked the Mini outside Dior and, still sitting in the passenger seat, I swung my legs out onto the pavement and was busy carefully oiling my skin so that it would shine dazzlingly when a very elegant elderly gentleman stopped in the street to voice his outrage: 'A little decency please, mademoiselle!' I answered him with my best smile. This fine gentleman was unaware that my career as a supermodel was on the line!

I wasn't the only one who had come to try her luck: the foyer was crawling with girls perched on their finest high heels, busy putting cream on their legs while they waited for their turn. I waited too, but not as long as I'd feared; everything was well organised here. And the girls who were sent by Flo were treated with respect and sometimes given priority, even at the big fashion houses. At the top of a stair-case, I was ushered into a huge room filled with racks sagging under the weight of clothes and tables covered in accessories. It was an Ali Baba's cave! A dresser handed me a pair of navy blue denim boots with massive heels: Galliano wanted to see us parade in the boots being used in the show. The good news was that they were a size 7, so I wouldn't have to go through the torture session again that I'd endured at Prada in Milan.

But it wasn't good news for everyone, apparently: a girl came out of the room where the designer was receiving us, yelling in English. She was furious because she'd tripped up in her size 7s; she took size 5 and was demanding to do the casting again in shoes of the right size. The assistant calmly explained to her that the boots only came in size 7, but the girl insisted on doing the casting again. I had never seen a model rebel like that, and so noisily too! And then suddenly I recognised the harpy: it was Bianca, a sublime Brazilian muse for Victoria's Secret who had inspired such dreams in me in New York! Looking at her closely, you had to say Photoshop worked wonders: she was 5 foot 8 inches at the very most and had short legs, wide hips and dreadful skin. And her behaviour was completely out of order. That was definitely one myth that had crumbled!

I remember having spoken about her to Louis in the plane to Milan and admitting that I would love to have that job. He replied with a hint of reproach in his voice: 'You're worth more than that, Victoire! All right, she earns $2 million a year, but you're a top haute couture model. Victoria's Secret is for the Yanks.' I hadn't really understood him at the time, but suddenly I saw what he meant! 'Those girls dream of doing Céline or Chanel. They'd be prepared to pay for the privilege, but it will never happen: they've had it. You can't compare apples and oranges, you know what I mean?'

John Galliano's assistant nevertheless let her go in once more, giving me a knowing glance as if to say sorry, and I could understand her: it was probably the quickest way to put an end to the situation. When little miss came back out, I entered in my turn. Perched on my star's boots, I steadily descended the three little steps that led down into a large room with beautiful parquet flooring. The room was very long and empty and at the end of it His Majesty Galliano was sitting regally behind a desk. He was faithful to his image: a ridiculously tall hat, white-blond hair, a big ring in his right ear, the Don Diego moustache and a huge crucifix hanging down over his shirt, which was unbuttoned a long way down and featured all the colours of the rainbow.

The woman sitting next to him asked me to come forward and so I went up and handed her my book under the completely impassive stare of the master. She opened the book, held it out to him and turned the pages for him. He didn't react at all – he was like a wax model at Madame Tussauds. 'Walk, please.' I turned round and my bottom was right in Galliano's face. I crossed the room again, taking care not to slip on the parquet, which wouldn't have been out of place at the Palace of Versailles, and back again I came. She took my comp card and gave me back my book with a smile. There was still no sign of life on John's face.

On my way out, I called Flo to tell her about it. 'Oh, Victoire, I forgot to tell you: he likes girls who walk very energetically, who take big strides and really plant their heels on the ground.' Too late, Galliano was a write-off then! Next it was off to Rue Saint-Honoré and Chanel. Perhaps I would have more luck with His Eminence Lagerfeld?

I didn't have the honour of being introduced to the man himself. I got there to find a crowd of some 200 girls, maybe more. Flo had told me to go straight up to see the casting director, who I had no trouble identifying: a small, slightly plump brunette who wasn't friendly at all. I said hello, introduced myself and said that I had been sent by Flo. She didn't reply, took my book, looked me up and down and gave me back my book without even taking my comp card or asking me to walk. So that was the end of that.

When I called Flo to report back, she wasn't surprised. 'I sent you there because it's Chanel, but Karl Lagerfeld doesn't like breasts. Your 32A is still too much for him. His number one model is Agnes. She's extremely flat-chested.'

Before I went home after this less than encouraging first day, Mum dropped me off at my grandparents', who I hadn't seen in ages. It was really lovely to see them again.

Nan took me in her arms and then stepped back to look at me. 'You're very beautiful, darling, but you're much too thin. Are you sure you're eating enough?'

I sidestepped the question by telling her that in a few days' time I would be doing a casting for Yves Saint Laurent, which was the very definition of French elegance in her eyes. Her face lit up. I knew that she had always admired his work, because when I was little she had told me once, when I was admiring her sketches, that she had studied at the École de la Chambre Syndicale de la Couture Parisienne, the private Paris fashion college, a few years after he had been there. In fact, her fashion sketches, which I'd often flicked through, were very reminiscent of what I knew of the great designer, as were the very elegant clothes that my darling grandmother always wore.

I spent a long time with Granddaddy telling him about New York, Milan and all my adventures in the wonderful world of fashion. He listened to me with a worried air. 'Make the most of your life, Victorinette. It goes by so quickly. And above all don't do what I did. Have the courage to do what you love.' I was worried by his state – he seemed so sad and tired. Before I left, I had a little look around the bathroom. It didn't take me long to find what I was looking for: in July in Marseille, Granddaddy had had serious stomach problems. A doctor eventually prescribed him some enemas, which relieved his symptoms almost immediately. If it had worked for him, it would surely work for me. My laxatives were having hardly any effect any more and I had 2 kilos I urgently needed to lose.

Earlier on, when Flo was telling me that I should have the legs of a goddess for Galliano, Léonce, an adorable booker who was as funny as he was crude, had interrupted us: 'Victoire, have you seen the legs you have? It's a disgrace to be so hot! I'd kill to have a body as unbelievable as yours.' Everybody laughed. 'And let me tell you, Victoire: we don't ask you to be fit, but it has to be said that you are well fit.' To me, it was amazing that they couldn't see how enormous I was.

I scrutinised my 'unbelievable body' in the mirror. My legs and arms were very slim, there was the thigh gap that I liked, and my ultra-flat stomach and my ribs. Then the bones of my pelvis and sternum, and my breasts which were still too big for Lagerfeld. I had hollow cheeks, which gave me huge eyes. I was pleased that they liked all that, but personally I couldn't understand it. They couldn't see the folds on my stomach if I didn't hold myself up absolutely straight, or the folds under my buttocks. My thighs were too flabby, as were my forearms. I had a double chin when I lowered my head. That was the effect of the 2 kilos I'd put on in Milan. They couldn't see that there was a danger I wouldn't be able to get into the clothes.

I spent some time with Léopold. We cuddled up together on his bed, told each other secrets and tickled each other. He said he was happy that I was home and I said he could have no idea just how happy I was to be home too. And then I went to bed with Plume, leaving open the door that separated my room from Alex's so that we could talk to each other as we fell asleep, just like we used to do.

The merry-go-round of the castings resumed at an infernal pace. Mum took me everywhere and we visited all the chic districts of Paris. She would wait for me in the car and then afterwards I'd tell her all about it. There was this guy, clearly on coke, who recognised my little Ralph Lauren dress and started to shriek: 'Oh, but what a good idea! I've never seen that – take a photo of her! You're so beautiful, I just want you, want you, want you for my show.' There was also the guy at Yves Saint Laurent – when I told Nan about him, she was going to be devastated. He was a huge vulgar oaf, buttoned up in a badly tailored suit and eyes hidden behind gold sunglasses, who chewed gum while he took photos with a huge camera in front of a large roll of white paper, like in Sergei's studio, and he kept saying, 'Look at me, sweetie. Be sensual.' I tripped in my high heels on the edge of his paper, which wasn't fixed to the ground. He immediately reacted, but not, as I thought, to stop me from falling, but rather to check that I hadn't torn his damn white canvas. 'For fuck's sake, watch the gear!' I reckoned things were screwed for Yves Saint Laurent too.

I also crossed paths again with Nikki and Ashley, the double act from Calvin Klein, at a completely chaotic casting. Like in New York, they picked girls out of the patiently expectant crowd as their crazy whims took them, without respecting at all the order in which we'd arrived. At Balenciaga, I met an adorable Dutch girl who was as thin as a stick and was studying at the École des Beaux-Arts and we had a chat about painting and museums while we were waiting our turn. Like me, it was her first season. She confessed in a whisper that she had to lie about her age: as soon as she said she was 20 instead of 27, everybody found her more attractive!

I bumped into Kate the Canadian and Mum ferried her around with me in her Mini when we had the same castings lined up. And then I met Maud, a diaphanous Dutch blonde who was very young and who confided in me, as if it were a big secret, that she'd found a trick to keep her figure in shape: she would eat one biscuit a day and nothing else. We took her along with us in the Mini too. They were very pleased to be pampered a bit by a mum, even if it wasn't their own mum.

At the casting at Paul & Joe, whose clothes I loved, I was welcomed enthusiastically by the designers (a young guy and a young woman), who thought I was 'exactly the image of the brand'. They wanted me to open their show and to do their campaign – at last it was happening to me! I appreciated their spontaneity and the fact that things could happen so straight-forwardly, even in that world.

I came out of the Ann Demeulemeester casting feeling a bit ashamed. I was in the process of leaving when one of the assistants caught up with me and said with a certain amount of embarrassment: 'Victoire, we really want to choose you. But you absolutely have to shave your arms – all those hairs are really too much ...'

That evening, before I shaved them, I went onto a medical website to find out what might cause abnormal hair growth. Top of the list of possible causes was anorexia. It was as if the body replaced fat with hair to protect itself from the cold. Anorexia? All right, I didn't eat much, but I did eat and I wasn't ill. I just watched myself, that was all, so that I could get into those damn clothes.

* * *

I felt very reticent about going to the Miu Miu fitting: I was really dreading that my tormentors at Prada and that witch Miuccia, who had given me such an unpleasant time of it in Milan, would be there. Fortunately, I had the pleasant surprise of running into Céleste, my Dutch friend who was living in New York and wanted, like me, to become an actress. We had plenty of time to resume our conversation while we were waiting for them to deign to call us. She told me that her man was a painter and she was his muse. It was my own dream to be so loved and idolised. She also told me about the relationship problems she'd had with a bashful lover who she couldn't bring herself to leave and who would follow her from city to city, even when she asked him not to. I had imagined that the life of a model would be more pleasant if you had a partner and I'd been dreaming that it would happen to me one day soon, but Céleste disabused me of the notion. According to her, it was hell living with someone if you were leading an existence like ours.

She also told me – in a low voice, because one didn't speak of such things – that a girl had died in the wings during one of the New York shows. 'She paraded as planned, but when she got backstage, she collapsed. The paramedics came but there was nothing they could do: she'd had a heart attack.' A heart attack, at 17? 'The stress, the fatigue, and of course we don't know what she was taking to keep going, do we? Personally, at the casting, I found you really very thin, half-starved even.' We changed the subject. I thought back to the day when I'd fainted on that New York crosswalk for lack of food, but I didn't share that with her. What was the point? We both knew, like everybody else, that none of the girls ate enough to satisfy their appetite during the shows.

And on the subject of food, Céleste shared a little detail that was very 'Prada': while we would have a disgusting buffet consisting of some dubious chicken drowning in an even more dubious sauce in aluminium boxes fit for the worst of canteens (I would never be able to understand how they could ask us to be sticklike but hardly ever lay on appropriate food for us), the team of designers was treated to a delicious buffet hidden in the next room. How very chic!

When my turn came, I was pleased to meet Olivier Rizzo again, the Belgian assistant to the witch, who had been so kind to me in Milan. Off we went together to get massacred by Miuccia. Apparently, the first dress he got me to try on wasn't suitable: she looked me up and down without a hello or any human warmth and then shook her head. Panicked, Olivier ran off to find another dress, which he begged me to put on as quickly as I could behind a folding screen put there for the purpose. I came before the learned judge again. With one finger, and still without a word, she pointed at a seam, which Olivier hastily rectified with a pin, being careful not to prick me. Then he attached a second and a third pin. She gestured to me to walk and so once again it was off, turn around and back to her. She gestured to me to turn around and I did so. And then I felt her push me in the back to get me to walk forward again. She really was an awful woman.

They started to speak in Italian and then they got up and left. Olivier just had time to explain to me with an apologetic expression that they couldn't think any more, that they were going to take a break and that I should wait. He didn't say for how long or anything else, not even if I could fit in lunch while they were gone. I got dressed and heard them leave. I pushed open the door to the adjoining room and I discovered the hidden buffet that Céleste had told me about. She hadn't been making it up: fruit, vegetables, meat and very fine and delicate fish prepared by one of the best caterers in Paris. I helped myself as an act of revenge, and too bad for the scales.

When I was lucky enough to get home in time, I prepared Léo's tea: big slices of toast with Nutella – much more than he could possibly eat, but I couldn't help myself. He'd eat them while telling me about life at school and listening to my tales as the queen of fashion.

At night, despite the exhausting days, I had trouble sleeping. I shouldn't have done, given that I was at home in my own bed with Plume and surrounded by all my loved ones, but I was afraid, and I no longer even knew what of. I'd always been afraid: that something terrible would happen, that I wouldn't be able to protect them all, that I would find myself alone and abandoned, that I wasn't what people wanted, that I wasn't loved any more and that they'd find a replacement for me.

Nobody could understand that, except perhaps Granddaddy. I think Granddaddy was afraid too, and of the same things as me.

When I was feeling really too frightened and the night was too long, I would get up without making a sound and go and make cakes in the kitchen, which I would then eat to overcome my fear, and perhaps my hunger too. I was back on an even keel, I was mastering my diet perfectly and the enemas were helping me to avoid putting on a single ounce. But when I wasn't doing anything, I couldn't help but feel hungry. I cooked muffins in trays of a dozen and I also made yoghurt and chocolate nuggets, again a dozen of each, and that kept me busy and provided the family with little hotel-style lunches. I delighted in the smell throughout the house and in seeing them feast. That filled me up for the day.

The Holy of Holies

I MET UP WITH RUSSELL MARSH once more at the Céline casting and we gave each other a big hug. He seemed as happy to see me again as I was to see him. I thanked him for saying so many nice things about me and for making sure that everybody was clamouring after me here. 'That's my job, Victoire. And it's a pleasure for me to encourage somebody like you.' He introduced me to his right-hand woman for Paris, Bouba, who was a pretty mixed-race girl from the Vosges and who was every bit as adorable and charming as he was. Russell had selected just a dozen models; he addressed all of them by their first name and he wanted to present them to his compatriot Phoebe Philo, the young and brilliant artistic director of the fashion house. Flo had briefed me well: going into Céline was akin to entering the holy of holies. It was an achievement restricted to girls who had been hand-picked and who corresponded to the very precise idea that Phoebe Philo had of fashion and of Parisian elegance. 'You'll see, it's the world of fashion as it used to be. You have to go through things stage by stage. It's another galaxy.'

I could sense that as soon as I walked in: they greeted me with warmth and respect in their huge modern offices situated in the district of Les Halles. There was no hysteria or agitation; everything was bright, calm, serene and elegant. Russell and Bouba received us in a pretty white room that served as the lounge. It was spacious and comfortable and in one corner they had prepared a refined buffet that was perfectly suited to our needs. The adjoining room had been turned into a fitting room, where we were able to put on a flesh-coloured body, a dressing gown and a pair of slippers before going back into the large lounge to wait our turn. When I came out, Russell winked and murmured, 'You've got a perfect body, Victoire. She's going to adore you.'

I had to wait another little while for him to come and get me. I followed him into a huge white room with blond parquet flooring which was lined with racks full of Céline garments in off-white, beige, brown and blue and in raw silk and moleskin, all of them splendid. At the far end of the room there was a massive mirror and, sitting behind two tables covered with fabrics, was a very pretty young woman, as delicate as a bird and with her hair pulled back into a ponytail, who was looking at me with her extremely light blue and distant eyes. Russell introduced me: 'Phoebe, this is Victoire, who is French.' I said hello and she gave me a little smile. I took off my dressing gown and she carefully looked me up and down. Russell asked me to walk, so I took off my slippers and crossed the room barefoot. They went off into a corner and spoke in low voices. My stomach tightened: something was wrong, they didn't like me; she didn't want me. Russell came back over to me and politely asked me to walk more slowly and to move my hips slightly so that I looked gentle and nonchalant. I walked towards her, she scrutinised me and then turned to Russell and gave him a little nod.

First stage passed! 'Come on, Victoire, we're going to try on some clothes.' Russell chose an outfit for me and I turned to Phoebe, who came up and made a few adjustments herself. Her delicate hands flitted around me like swallows, hardly touching me as she spoke very quietly to her assistant. Before positioning her needles, she slipped a finger under the fabric to make sure she didn't prick me! It was all gentle, light, tranquil and unbelievably respectful. Then it was on to the second outfit and a second session of adjustments which was just as delicate. She stepped back to contemplate her work and smiled at me: 'Goodbye, Victoire, and thank you very much.'

I came out of that session on a cloud. I adored Russell and I adored that woman.

An hour later, Flo called me: 'Well done, Victoire! I had Russell on the phone and he told me that Phoebe Philo just adored you! Wouldn't it be incredible if you did the Céline show? You realise it's *the* thing that everybody dreams of?' I didn't realise, no, but I could understand why. She explained that the next stage would be hair and make-up and that Russell would no doubt do his best to ensure that I was involved, because that would considerably increase my chances of being chosen for the show. She told me too that

I'd been chosen for the Miu Miu show and so she'd said no to Paul & Joe, whose show was on the same day at the same time and who had booked me too, as they'd promised me. I was extremely disappointed – I liked them as much as I detested Miuccia. 'Victoire, what you like is neither here nor there. The key thing is that it gets you work. Miu Miu is Prada, and you don't say no to Prada.'

It was great working with Flo because she spoke to me adult to adult. She might have been the one making the decisions, but at least things happened quickly and everything was organised and precise. It was very professional. I was discovering another way of working which suited me much better. Seb did everything behind my back as if I were his possession, announcing the schedule higgledy-piggledy and at the last minute, which drove me crazy. And now I was driving him crazy: I'd blocked him on my phone, I didn't answer his calls any more and I didn't even listen to his messages. As a result, he'd started harassing my parents, who had built an unbreachable rampart between him and me. He told Dad that they were in the process of ruining my career and that it was criminal. And then after a while, he got fed up and we didn't hear from him again, or at least I didn't.

For the time being, my 'career' didn't really seem to be in 'ruins': I was starting my Paris season with a show for Taralis at the Palais de Tokyo, squeezed into ripped black jeans, a camouflage short-sleeved shirt buttoned up to the neck and soldier's boots, all in an end-of-days atmosphere shot through with the sinister chiming of the bells of the apocalypse. I followed that up with Damir Doma, a Belgo-Croatian designer who I didn't even have a casting for – it was Samuel Drira, the French designer who had summoned me in the middle of the night in New York, who had been in charge of selecting the models. He chose me automatically, without even seeing me again. We paraded in one of the halls of the Museum of Natural History amid an array of fabulous minerals.

Next, at the Cordeliers Convent, I had to wear the very hazardous, exclusively leather 'graphic abstractions' of Ann Demeulemeester, who had taken the trouble to make a map of the catwalk for us to make sure we didn't walk in the wrong direction! Doubtless she thought that these very carefully selected bodies were not equipped with brains.

Between the shows, the castings continued; everything was very condensed here. I failed the Sonia Rykiel casting, because I didn't know that she hated as much as I did those models who walk in a straight line and look miserable – I hadn't taken the risk of showing her my personality. I didn't dare to slam the door on the Vuitton casting either, where they asked us to present ourselves wearing only a thong and high heels in an atmosphere that was heavy and stifling. I loved the Castelbajac casting, which was as vibrant and colourful as the walls of the room to which we were summoned. And I was desperate to be chosen for Wunderkind, which was the brand of the Dutch designer Wolfgang Joop, who had created a magnificent collection, very reminiscent of Tim Burton's universe and themed around Alice in Wonderland.

I took a break to take part in the hair and make-up session at Céline, which Flo was so hopeful about – 'Great, Victoire! I'm telling you, you're going to get it!' – and which was almost a fairy tale compared to the violence of the session at Prada. The make-up artists and hairstylists were all French and they were gentle, charming and considerate, in keeping with the image of the major fashion house. Everything unfolded in an atmosphere of calm serenity. And Phoebe Philo greeted me with a 'Hello, Victoire,' and a really lovely smile.

On that particular day I met another French girl, Suzie, whose thinness made an impression on me and in fact genuinely frightened me. She told me that she'd been in this profession for four years and, despite all her efforts, she'd never managed to get her hip measurement down below 36 inches. 'There's nothing I can do about it – my skeleton is too wide. And so they never choose me for the shows: I can hardly get into a size 6, so you can imagine what it's like with a size 4.' I was speechless when she confessed that sweet little Solène, her booker at Elite, had said to her: 'The best thing for you to do is to find yourself a rich man and marry him.'

Meanwhile, I had been chosen for the Miu Miu fitting – an entire day at the mercy of the witch! But in fact it was in striking contrast to the last time: fortunately Olivier, her right-hand man and my guardian angel, was putting in the needles under her instructions and so I escaped the worst. He even kindly invited me to have lunch; I got official access to the buffet that I had raided a few days earlier. He defended his boss as best he could: 'You know, she's a wonderful person. She perhaps comes across as a bit harsh, but she's really very talented. And the thing is, she's a stellar designer, she has a status to maintain, and she can't be seen to be accessible. That's all part of the game.' I thought back to the delicate elegance of Phoebe, but I didn't dare contradict him: he'd been working with, and enduring, Miuccia for ten years, so there must have been something there that appealed to him.

On the evening of 2 October, I was at home preparing tea for Léo when Flo rang. 'I've got some good news and some bad news – which do you want first?' I always preferred to save the best till last. 'Well then, I know you're going to be disappointed, but I've cancelled Wunderkind tomorrow, because you've been chosen for Vuitton, which is happening at the same time. Keep your phone close to you and I'll ring you at dawn to give you the details.' Oh no! I had so wanted to take a stroll through wonderland and I so didn't want to see those louts again who had made us go topless to assess us. 'But you've been chosen for the Leonard, Vanessa Bruno and Collette Dinnigan shows.' OK, that wasn't so bad. Together with the ones I'd already done, that would make for a respectable season.

'And above all, Victoire, you're also booked for … Alexander McQueen and CÉLINE!!!'

Into the Light

WHEN I ARRIVED AT THE VENUE for the Céline show, the technicians were putting the finishing touches to the hall, where they had constructed a very large, completely white space through which a catwalk snaked, lined with tiered seating. The wings were hidden behind a false wall, where the team was busying itself around Phoebe Philo, who was calm and focused. I was greeted like a distinguished guest by the stage manager. 'Hello, Victoire, how are you? Follow me! Phoebe has prepared a present for you.' In my allotted place, and in those of all the other models, there was a huge wrapped present with my name on it. When I opened it, I found a sumptuous bag from the new collection – *the* bag that all the fashionistas would be dreaming of possessing when it went on sale. Phoebe had chosen it specially for me – we were each given a different model – and had slipped in a little handwritten message to explain her choice: 'For Victoire, the elegance and character of the Parisian woman.' It was already a wonderful gift to be one of the lucky few doing the show, and now on top of this we were going home with a collector's item!

I got to know my dresser Lola, who was stunned that I chatted to her. 'You know, most of the models treat us as if we don't exist. Or worse … Follow my gaze!' Two chairs further along, Agnes, the darling of the designers and Karl Lagerfeld's muse, was looking as blasé unwrapping her huge Céline bag as I had looked amazed when I was unwrapping mine. Lola winked at me. Clearly Agnes was maintaining her status as an elite model by cultivating that superior and condescending attitude that seemed to be de rigueur in the wonderful world of fashion. I told Lola that I was constantly amazed to see the models, who were treated so badly by the designers, stylists and casting directors, in turn treating the make-up artists, hairstylists and dressers so badly. It was as if you had to perpetuate the tradition, making them endure what we ourselves endured.

Agnes was staring at me, perhaps because I too couldn't help staring at her very bizarre body. All her bones were sticking out of her skin, which sported tattoos all over. She was topless and all that remained of her non-existent breasts were pierced nipples. That, together with her endless untoned arms and legs, ultimately gave her an extraordinary, almost monstrous appearance. She was fascinating. 'You wouldn't believe how she treats us,' whispered Lola.

We lined up in the order we were due to go on and Phoebe inspected us thoroughly, rectifying tiny details in her bird-like way. I was just behind my friend Céleste. 'That's not right,' said Phoebe, 'could you swap tops?' I gave my white top to

Céleste, who gave me her blue one. Phoebe's unerring eye had got it right: it was much better that way round.

Then silence, music, lights. Russell had warned me: 'For this show, don't walk too fast. Everything has to be gentle, even your gaze.' I walked amid the unbelievable crowd of spectators (Carine Roitfeld, Anna Wintour and other personalities from *Vogue*), following the undulating curves of the catwalk in Phoebe's soft and flowing clothes. I was focused and happy, genuinely happy!

At the end of the show after the applause, Phoebe finally relaxed. I got a chance to talk to her and to thank her for her wonderful gift. 'You're wonderful too, Victoire.' And then I went to embrace Russell, without whom none of this would have happened.

When I left, I was greeted by a small crowd of photographers and some highly excited bloggers, who begged me to pose with them as if I were Marilyn Monroe and asked me what I was wearing. Seb had warned me: 'Never tell the truth, you have to keep the dream alive!' And so I told them that I had found my 100 per cent H&M blue cotton outfit 'in a second-hand shop in the Marais' and my shoes at Aldo in New York. As for my brand-new Céline bag, it spoke for itself. 'Something vintage and something classy is what creates the magic balance in fashion, baby': on that point at least, Seb had been right.

The next day I did the Leonard show on a fluorescent pink catwalk beneath Alexandre-III bridge, which had been transformed into a multicoloured set. I was topless in a beige thong when a TV crew turned up backstage with their camera! It was rather a strange way to treat models, and there were other surprises in store for me: after the show, which was all veils and flowery patterns, Leonard's guests spilled over into our changing rooms like a human tide in order to feast to their heart's delight on our undressed bodies, as if we were part of the spectacle!

Mum picked me up outside and we sped off, jumping several red lights (I wasn't about to relive the Francesco Scognamiglio episode in Milan!), to the Palais de Chaillot for the Vanessa Bruno show. She greeted the models in person as if we were her friends. 'Victoire! How are you? How did you get here?' I told her that Mum was waiting for me in her Mini. 'Oh, bring her in! I'm sure she'd be pleased to see you parade!' So a delighted Mum joined us backstage and was there with me when I discovered the pretty bag that was waiting for me as a gift. And then I paraded to a punchy soundtrack, my heart full of joy, beneath the Eiffel Tower and in front of Mum! In the large fluorescent orange bag, which was bound to go down a storm in the women's magazines the following summer, I found an envelope containing a €500 voucher and a little handwritten message: 'You're superb! Thank you to my find of the season for doing my show!'

The following day I had an appointment at the sublime Hôtel Meurice in front of an audience of celebrities and starlets to present the princess dresses – satin, lace and rhinestone – of the Australian Collette Dinnigan. I found myself surrounded by a horde of Russian models who were ready to trample on anyone who tried to edge them out of the photo. Mum was allowed in too. 'Oh, sweetie, your mother is so nice!' And to think that Seb used to loudly proclaim that under no circumstances should I be accompanied by my mother, because 'they' hate that! Whether at D' Management, at Vanessa Bruno or here at the Hôtel Meurice, 'they' all seemed delighted to welcome her with open arms and were touched to see us together.

Two days later I turned up at the Musée de l'Homme for the Alexander McQueen show, my heart pounding: I loved this designer and Flo had said that doing his show could open a lot of doors for me in future seasons. Mum dropped Alex and me off at the entrance: I'd decided to try to get him in so that he got to see at least one of my shows, but, despite my pleading, the security staff firmly refused to allow him back-stage: see you at the exit in a little while, then!

Amid all the hustle and bustle in the wings, Sarah Burton, the English designer and former lieutenant of Alexander McQueen who was presenting her first collection since the death of the master, was biting her nails and desperately look-ing for someone who could wear dress number 6. 'Would you like to try, Victoire? Don't worry if you can't get into it. There's always the dress you wore at the casting, but I really adore this one. We made a mistake and made it too small: nobody can get into it.'

The dresser and I set about the challenge and, miracle of miracles, I managed to slip into the complicated get-up of the short little dress, with its flounces and colourful pattern, without too much trouble. It was tightly cinched at the waist with a sophisticated leather shackle with gold buckles. I couldn't believe it myself: enormous though I was, I'd managed it! Shout it from the rooftops: I was the only one who could get into dress number 6! My joy lasted for as long as it took me to sit down – which exceptionally was allowed, because the dress was so short that there was no danger of me creasing it – and put on the incredible matching shoes, half normal boots and half ski boots, that completed my outfit. They were a size 6 with 7-inch heels – a nightmare.

I got out of the dress and shoes to go and get my hair and make-up done and that's when I realised it was much worse than a nightmare: I immediately recognised my Milanese tormentors from Prada. And they hadn't changed: not a word, not a glance, totally absorbed in their conversation. They attacked my scalp with a hair straightener with their customary brutality, which was enough to bring tears to my eyes. They showed no consideration towards me and offered no apologies.

But the result was incredible: my skull was on fire but my hair was perfectly braided, my face was subtly whitened, my waist was clamped with the buckles and snap links of my dress, my nails were painted with golden motifs and my feet were held in the vice-like grip of my shoes. I looked like a sublime Amazonian warrior ready for battle. A few metres away from me, the young American elite model Karlie Kloss, squeezed into the most beautiful dress of the collection, was moving everyone out of the way so that she could practise walking!

When I went out into the light with my undulating gait to the sound of grandiose music, I couldn't feel my tortured feet any more or my slaughtered skull. I was a queen – a goddess parading in the heart of the Musée de l'Homme who had been made larger than life by a wonderful designer who was offering the public a spectacle of staggering beauty.

The show came to an end and I went backstage to get the dresser to help me out of those shoes and put me out of my misery. We were still at the task when the scrum of photographers erupted into the dressing rooms. It was unbelievable! And amid the lenses and flashbulbs I recognised Alex who, with a big smile, was snapping me like a true pro – amazingly he'd managed to get in! I quickly got dressed while he described how he'd managed to pass himself off as a photographer, thanks to his huge camera and his laid-back demeanour. I took him to the buffet to mingle with the beautiful people to round off the party. I sidled up to Sarah Burton, who was deep in conversation with a very beautiful woman dressed entirely in McQueen, to thank her for the extraordinary experience that I'd just had thanks to her. They both turned towards me smiling and I recognised the actress Salma Hayek. Stammering a bit, I told Sarah how happy I'd been to do her show and to wear her sublime debut collection. When Salma replied, to the wide-eyed amazement of my brother, 'You're the one who's sublime,' I felt myself filling up with joy and pride.

I watched Alexis tucking into the delicious petits fours which my bastard little voice had prohibited me from touching, but I did allow myself a glass of champagne to toast this beautiful show with him. And then we went home to recount our McQueen afternoon to the others.

The Miu Miu show was closing the spring/summer season that year in the gardens of the Palais-Royal, which had been privately hired out and covered with an immense tent for the occasion. Having once more passed through the hands of my Milanese tormentors, I was very happy to see Olivier Rizzo again, who embraced me as if we'd been friends for ever under the attentive and irritated gaze of Agnes, who was getting ready two seats further along. When my dresser appeared with my shoes, which were spectacular see-through sandals with green and pink stripes and fluorescent laces, Olivier intervened: 'Let me do it!' And so there was I sitting on my chair and Miuccia Prada's right-hand man was at my feet putting on those implausible stilts! He was setting about the laces of the left foot when I caught a reflection in the mirror and for a fraction of a second I glimpsed the furious expression of Agnes, who was observing the scene. She was jealous! I saw her immediately take it out on her poor dresser, who she dismissed with a brisk tap. I discreetly described the scene to my trusty knight, who murmured, 'Don't worry about it,' before getting up and innocently turning round to Agnes: 'Hello darling, how are you? Let me help you with your shoes …'

* * *

Half an hour later, my first season came to an end in the gardens of the Palais-Royal amid thunderous applause for Miuccia Prada, the witch of the catwalks. I took a glass of champagne over to Mum, who Bouba had got in as a guest, so that she could enjoy a bit of the backstage atmosphere before taking me home. I was both happy and unhappy, exhausted and galvanised. And in truth, completely lost …

The Photo Shoots

IT WAS A MASSIVE RELIEF, before going back to work, to have two days off in which to do the things that normal people do when they have time off. I spent a long afternoon catching up with my friend Sophie, who I hadn't seen for far too long. She didn't actually reproach me, but I knew that she found it difficult to accept that we'd had so little contact in recent months. I thought to myself that you had to be a model to understand what a model's life was like. I also went for a walk in the Parc Monceau with my grandparents and spent an evening with my cousin and his friends, one of whom performed in a lot of comedy sketches and improvisational theatre. I helped Léo with his homework, went to a matinée with Alexis the film buff and had a siesta with my little Plume …

I did actually go to the agency for a little party to celebrate the end of fashion week. Flo greeted me with a big smile and was full of enthusiasm. Vladimir also came over to embrace me and congratulate me: 'Well done, Victoire. You went down a storrrm! Twenty-two shows, including Céline, Miu Miu and Alexander McQueen. For a firrrst season, that's a verrry rrrare thing! Febrrruary is going to be epic, my darrrling! They're alrrready starting to call.'

Flo and I found a quiet corner to review the upcoming schedule. Now that the fashion shows were over, it was the photo shoot season for the front or inside pages of the magazines or for the various brands that had noticed me in recent weeks and wanted to include me in their lookbook, the catalogue for presenting their collection to the print media and the retail buyers. And all the while we would be waiting for the jackpot: a contract for a brand campaign, which I would represent on posters and in ad pages. I had heard enough girls dreaming of that in the queues at the castings to know that it was these much trumpeted campaigns that made a model's fortune, and that of their agencies.

Speaking of agencies, Flo kept on hinting that it was about time that I clarified the situation with Seb and chose Elite as my primary agency. I could see that she also wouldn't be averse to the idea of me reconsidering my commitments to Silent and D' Management and I knew that she was right. Seb had introduced me to them and both Silent and D' Management had been kind to me, but I wasn't obliged to be dumbly loyal to people just because I owed them something or because I liked them: 'It's business, Victoire. It's not about good intentions.' While she waited for me to get around to tackling these issues – I would have to talk to my parents to get their opinion and advice – Flo went through my schedule for the coming weeks: photo shoots in Paris, Milan ('Oh *no*, not Milan!') and London, test photos with photographers selected by the agency to pad out my book, and reshoots in London. 'Not to mention all the other stuff that's going to come in!'

I wasn't sure if I really wanted to do all that. I was tired, I felt cold all the time and now that I wasn't living life in the fast lane, I was also starting to feel hungry all the time. And I was getting bored too: what was I going to do between now and February fashion week? What goal could I aim for, now that I'd achieved the first goal I'd set myself? I knew this was stupid: for several weeks I'd been dreaming of slowing down, having time to myself and catching my breath a bit, and now that I could, instead of taking advantage I felt empty and sad, very sad.

What was I going to do with my life?

After two days' rest, I started the photo shoots. The first was for Busnel on a sunny day down by the Canal Saint-Martin. A photographer, an assistant and a designer from the brand were there to help me coordinate and put on the outfits and there was also a woman to do my hair and make-up. It was a small crew and we took four hours in the bright sunshine to wrap up all the pictures for the forthcoming collection. The very sweet photographer encouraged me to take the initiative: 'Suggest things to me. Invent situations, toy with me and with the clothes!' I did what I could, but I got bored very quickly. Fashion, when there wasn't the stage fright of the shows, the buzz of the crowd, the flashbulbs, the set, the music and the designer's stress, was suddenly distinctly less interesting!

The following morning it was off to the Marais for a photo shoot for *Untitled*, a cultural magazine whose existence I wasn't even aware of! The photographer Amira Fritz greeted me warmly and Lotta, the Dutch designer, transformed me into a curious creature who was half childlike and half disturbing in a tulle dress and striped socks, complemented by really bizarre make-up and a very striking backcombed hairdo. It was in this rather remarkable get-up that I got the metro with them to the Bois de Boulogne. It was a fun and intriguing adventure and would be something to tell the boys about that evening! As I watched Amira work and looked at the proofs that she showed me on her screen, I understood that she was composing strange, slightly baroque and magical fairy-tale images with the woods and me as the leading characters. It was meticulous and time-consuming work where every detail counted: a little flower, the position of my fingers on the trunk, the fold of the tulle on my thigh, the shape of the branch and the shadow it cast … The whole thing took hours. I was cold as usual, a bit more than usual in fact – it was after all autumn and we were in the Bois de Boulogne.

At around one o'clock, the assistant went off to buy some sausages and chips in the little hut she'd spotted at the previous crossroads. Amira held out a portion to me which I declined, instead getting an apple out of my bag. With a smile, she insisted, 'Don't tell me you're on a diet! I'm against diets. Eat some chips, Victoire! You're much too thin.' I said that I really couldn't, and I felt fear gnawing away in my stomach. 'I'm not asking you to be fat, just normal. A couple of chips aren't going to make you explode!'

And yet the very idea was making my brain explode and my bastard little voice was yelling at me. Didn't she know that chips were the ultimate poison, that they were death, my death? She was against 'models on diets', but what she didn't consider for a moment was why I was there and not Madeleine or Olympe. How did I end up at Elite and why had her client chosen me for her to photograph?

She told me that a few years ago she had worked with a model who had been called a 'fat cow' by a casting director even though she was completely scrawny. After giving up the profession, her body had been so knackered that it took her five years before she managed to conceive. I kept quiet, ate my apple and then did some more posing. My teeth were chattering and I wanted to go home.

I was present, but I had the feeling that I was absent, absent from myself.

When I got home that evening, I begged Mum to call Flo: the next day, I was due to fly off to Milan for two days to do a shoot for an article in a women's magazine and to feature on their front cover. I really didn't want to go back there and find myself all alone in a hotel again. I was afraid and I didn't think I could manage it.

Mum put the phone on speaker and Flo sounded annoyed: 'Why doesn't Victoire call herself?'

'Don't be hard on her, Florence. She's very tired. She got very cold in the Bois de Boulogne and is resting.'

'I can't cancel tomorrow's shoot, I can't do that to the client.'

'But don't you think one day would suffice? She could leave early in the morning and get the last plane back.'

Mum was brilliant! An hour later, Flo emailed to confirm that my plane tickets had been changed and that I'd leave at dawn and return that evening.

And so I did go to Milan and the day spent with an attentive and friendly team was calm and relaxed. I posed in my sublime light blue silk dress from Dior and everything was easy and straightforward. I even had time to pop into D' Management and say hello to Francesca and the team before I got the last plane back home to my own bed.

Before I went off to the agency, the photographer had shown me the photos and I watched him begin to retouch them: in a few clicks, he plumped up my cheeks, thighs and breasts and erased the bones of my sternum to give me an attractive cleavage. So that was how things worked: we lost kilo upon kilo so that they chose us, only for them to put it all back on as they saw fit.

But there was no arguing with the before and after test: I had to admit that I was prettier with all those curves.

Back home, they asked me how the day had gone and I changed the subject. I was fed up with talking about this profession.

The Fat Cow

IT WAS DREADFUL. Rotten countryside, rotten weather and I hadn't slept a wink all night. I'd been stressing ever since Flo had called me to say that I had a photo session with a male model for Calvin Klein – incredibly, the double act who had ignored me for all their shows had suddenly remembered me and demanded me urgently – at a country house in the middle of nowhere. I'd seen in the magazines what those kinds of photos could be like: the girl half naked hugging the naked torso of the guy and swooning. Or else the guy's nose in the girl's cleavage, or loved-up poses, lips touching. I wasn't interested and I wouldn't be able to deal with that kind of situation.

As planned, Mum dropped me off at eight o'clock at the Gare du Nord, where I was supposed to be meeting the other model and the team, but they failed to spot me and left without me. How nice of them! I called Flo, who told me to take a taxi and so I spent an hour and a half on my own on the road, wondering what was in store for me at the other end.

Damien Blottière, the photographer, was adorable. He gave me a really warm welcome, apologised profusely for his team not waiting for me and immediately reimbursed the taxi. He showed me around the house, indicated the rooms where I could have a rest or get changed and introduced me to the others in the large living room which had been trans-formed into a studio. There was Nicolas, the really nice hair-stylist I'd worked with on the Silent video in Paris before heading off to the fashion weeks; Sergio, an exuberant South American make-up artist – very much the 'my darling, my darling' type – who was absolutely adorable; the dresser sent by Calvin Klein; the agent of the model who would pose with me, who was a tall, bizarre and mysterious type who didn't say a word and struck me as rather unsavoury; and finally there was Christian the model, a very young German who was incredibly thin and couldn't have been more than 16, who had very blue eyes and looked like an animal in a trap. I instantly felt relieved – the guy didn't have the presence to do the kind of sexy photos I'd been dreading – but worried too, because clearly he was as much of a novice as me.

I waited for ages and ages while they set their stuff up and moved things around. They filmed Christian on his own while I sat by the buffet and watched. I was beginning to feel really very hungry. I could smell the ham on the plate just under my nose. God knows how long it had been since I'd last eaten ham – three months, maybe four.

I used to really like ham and I felt like eating ham then and there. An irrepressible yearning welled up from inside and invaded my brain. I began to salivate, and to debate with myself: Ham's out of the question – too salty and too fatty. In fact, when Christian wanted to have a slice just now, his agent rapped him on the fingers to stop him. Ham is forbidden. If you want to eat, eat fruit or vegetables. Look, there are some tomatoes and even a cucumber. But no ham, it's full of protein and will make you fat.

Yes, but Flo said that for the photo shoots we could put a bit of weight back on. Going up to size 6 wasn't a problem as long as I got back to size 4 for the February fashion week in three months' time. I can go easy for a bit.

But if you go easy, don't eat ham but the really nice stuff! Cheese, the *niniches* of La Baule or Nan's apple tart and stew. Granddaddy's *rillettes* on toast. Or else some brioche. Mmm, brioche with redcurrant jam. After all the effort you've made, surely you're not going to cave in for a slice of ham?

I rolled up a slice of ham and bit into it with delight – it was delicious. I took a second, a third, a fourth, a fifth slice.

I have to get away from this buffet, I told myself.

Christian walked past with his worried air and headed towards the kitchen. I followed him, figuring that if we were going to pose together, we might as well get to know each other. When I walked in, he was eating a lump of sugar. He turned round and jumped when he saw me, as if he'd been caught committing a terrible crime. He looked terrified and begged me not to say anything to his agent, and of course I promised not to. How could you get into such a state just because you were caught eating a lump of sugar? I tried to get him talking a bit as he looked in such a bad state, but he completely clammed up and I could understand that. Even though he was a beginner, he must already have learned enough in this business to know that it was better not to trust anyone.

My turn still hadn't come and so I went to see Damien, who was adjusting the settings on his camera. A glance at his computer screen revealed that his work was absolutely incredible. He digitally cropped and shaped the photos he'd taken to turn them into minutely detailed and intriguing works of art. He summoned Christian and I returned to the buffet. Not the crisps, nor the cured sausage. But the dried apricots were still acceptable – they were fruits, after all.

And so I ate the apricots. The entire packet, in fact, in less than ten minutes. A quarter of an hour later I was doubled up in pain. My digestive system was making me pay violently for this monstrous intake of food, which it had become completely unused to. And what a bloody idiot – I hadn't thought to bring my laxatives. I lay down on the bed in one of the rooms Damien had shown me when I arrived and I went to sleep.

When the dresser woke me up, I was feeling slightly better. She handed me the first outfit and I got undressed in front of the large mirror on the wall of the bedroom. When I saw my body, I gasped: it was completely deformed. Above the beige thong, my stomach had swollen appallingly. It looked like a ball balanced on my thighs, which as a result looked impossibly thin. I looked like the little starving Africans you see on TV. The dresser's eyes focused on my navel and then slid up to my face. My heart began to race as it dawned on me that I might not be able to get into the clothes. 'Are you OK, Victoire?' I told her that I'd eaten too much and that I had a very bad stomach ache. She put away the very slim-fitting little blue dress she'd intended for me and handed me instead a massive white cape dress that you could have got a cow into.

Nobody said anything and nobody saw anything. Damien got me to pose, white-faced as I was, in my white dress in front of a white wall. He was sweet with me and I followed his instructions like an automaton. He didn't notice that I just wasn't there.

I wasn't anywhere, I no longer existed.

When I got home, I took an enema and I spent all night crapping to expel that day's food orgy. 'That'll teach me.'

The following morning, I got on the scales with trepidation. I was sure that I'd put on a kilo, maybe two. Five slices of ham and a packet of dried apricots was like a time bomb.

The scales read 47.2. I hadn't put on a single gram. That unpleasant day was ultimately going to open up new vistas for me ...

Life as a Clothes Hanger

IT WAS AS IF THE SLICES OF HAM at Damien's photo shoot had awakened my appetite and nothing could be done to suppress it again. It became a bottomless pit. Since it didn't make me fat, I started to eat again, but healthily and never in front of other people. I was ashamed, as if I were doing something very private or very bad. I ate fruit and steamed vegetables, chicken and fish. When Dad noticed what was on my plate, he was reassured. What he didn't know was that to complement my new diet, I was taking laxatives in the morning and an enema every evening. I spent half my life in the toilet, my stomach hurt and my bum hurt, and I felt like vomiting all the time, but at least I didn't feel hungry any more, or a lot less hungry at any rate.

I did put on 3 kilos, though, and initially I saw it as a disaster – my nasty little voice nearly drove me nuts. But eventually I grew comfortable with it. If I was around 50 kilos, I could get into a size 6 and a size 8, which for the photo shoots was ideal. After Christmas I would go back onto a strict diet to get back down to a size 4.

Nobody noticed anything at the agency. Mind you, they all had a laugh at my expense because Damien had given me €200 for my taxi back and I handed Flo the €35 left over so that she could give it back to him. They couldn't believe it – they said they'd never heard of a model giving back unspent money on what she'd been advanced and that all of Paris would be talking about it. It became the big wisecrack of the week: I was *that girl* who said hello, goodbye, please sir, thank you madam and, to cap it all, gave back the money she was advanced! Well, if it made them laugh, bully for them.

A model's life is not a party beyond the fashion shows.

When I didn't have any photo shoots, my main activity was doing the rounds of the editorial offices of the women's magazines to do beauty shoots: photos of make-up, skin and hair. And they would talk to me about make-up, skin and hair as if they were the most important subjects in the world.

I was getting bored.

I did do a show for one little-known designer in a dark theatre amid suited and booted IBM executives. It was a dinner and they sat there eyeing us up as if we were the dessert. When I got home, I felt like vomiting.

I was chosen too for the Sonia Rykiel lookbook. I was very happy to go there, because I liked that brand a lot and also the woman herself, her daughter and their story, but of course I didn't get to see them. I was received by a photographer who didn't even say hello to me and I spent four hours putting on clothes and posing in silence against a white backdrop, changing and then doing it all over again.

When I got out of sessions like that, I felt totally empty, hollow and transparent, with the IQ of a clothes hanger. Lagerfeld was right: what else were we, ultimately?

I went to London for two days for the lookbook and presentation of Gap, who had chosen me on Russell Marsh's recommendation. I took the Eurostar with an excellent bottle of champagne picked out by Dad in my bag. I dropped in to see Russell at his office to present it to him and to thank him for everything he'd done for me. I was so pleased to see him again, and clearly he was pleased to see me too. He told me that it was rare in this world to meet girls who were 'cultured and well brought up'. I didn't dare tell him that what appealed to him was laughable to most of the people I associated with. He wished me good luck and set up an appointment with me for February. 'You'll see, it will be extraordinary!'

I headed off to Regent's Park, where I posed for three hours for a photographer who was about as friendly as a crocodile and who shouted, 'Next!' after each pose. Among the models present was the little German whose thinness had scared me in Milan. I know it sounds odd, but I felt relieved that she wasn't dead.

I don't know if it was because I was eating more or because I was working less, but I felt that I was starting to think clearly again for the first time in months, and I was none too sure that this was good for my career.

When the lookbook was wrapped up, we were invited to 'move towards the buffet' to have lunch before the guests arrived for the afternoon presentation. It was a splendid buffet, worthy of Russell Marsh! And miracle of miracles, for the first time ever I decided that I was actually entitled to make the most of it. I delighted in helping myself to a slice of courgette tart. The pastry was crusty and the filling was both tasty and creamy – I savoured every mouthful, right down to the last crumb. I liked eating, I adored eating, it was *good* to eat. And you can shut up, you bastard little voice – leave me in peace just this once.

For dessert, I had a bowl of raw fruit – one shouldn't take things too far, after all …

All this gave me the energy to find out, and then to endure, what a 'presentation' was in the world of Gap. You take some models (living, human ones), you dress them in clothes from the latest collection, you put them into pairs of boy and girl, you put them on a little podium and you ask them not to move while the guests mill around, chat, tuck into the buffet and, if they so desire, inspect the said clothes close up. I was lucky enough to be paired with a very nice Parisian guy who lived just up the road from me, which meant we were able to get through this rather surreal experience by chatting about our respective home lives. Until, that is, one of the Gap representatives came over and brought us back into line: the models weren't supposed to talk to anyone, let alone to each other. According to her, that would spoil the presentation of the collection. We shut up until her back was turned. It was a dog's life, this life as a clothes hanger!

The next day, I weighed myself and realised that the previous night's enema had not been enough to erase the traces of the courgette tart: 50.5 kilos. Five hundred grams in one go. I wouldn't eat another thing until I was back down to 50.

Two days later, I hooked up again with my dear Olivier Rizzo, who had recommended me to Willy Vanderperre, his photographer friend who was also Belgian, for a photo shoot in Paris. We hugged and exchanged news, and then it was the usual routine: hair, make-up, hanging around. One hour, two, three, having to put up with an unbearable model who shared every little detail of her life, who knew everything there was to know, who handed down advice and who babbled and bragged endlessly. I just wanted her to shut up and I also wanted something to eat. I'd been on my apple diet for two days to be sure of getting into the clothes.

I really did feel hungry.

For lunch we were allocated the usual low-rent buffet – meat in a sauce, pastry tarts, fruit with syrup – while the team were served up small low-calorie organic dishes and all the other appropriate foods. I sidled up to Olivier so that I could get some of the special menu beneath the furious gaze of the studio manager. I just managed to poach a portion of steamed chicken before she wrapped everything up, staring at me as if I were pulling off the bank heist of the century.

The afternoon went on for ever – we just waited and waited and waited. The chatterbox was chattering away. At around three o'clock, Olivier came to tell me it would be my turn 'soon'. A few moments later, a very tall girl with a large mouth appeared; she looked exhausted and exasperated. I recognised Lindsey Wixson, the catwalk star, who the team had just greeted with the respect befitting her status. She had to go through the make-up, hair and hanging around routine just like the rest of us. Sometimes even the luxury clothes hangers had to wait too. Lindsey got agitated, stood up, sat down, got up again and paced up and down. And then suddenly, without a word, she began to cry, discreetly at first, but then she burst out sobbing uncontrollably.

I understood, because I'd been there myself. I thought back to that day in Milan when I too had cracked up beneath the triumphant gaze of the Russian wasps. I'd thought to myself that I'd never be an elite model, because the elite models never cracked up, but here was proof that they did.

The team looked after her well, getting her to sit down, consoling her and redoing her make-up. They assured her that they understood that she was tired, what with this crazy life, the time difference and the endless flights, and they let her go in front of me so that she could get back quickly to the hotel and rest.

It was gone five when I finally found myself in the presence of the photographer with the same make-up I'd had for the Miu Miu show, wavy hair and an attractive white silk shirt that was fully unbuttoned. He smiled at me, spoke to me and encouraged me. I did what he asked me and I toyed with him. It was free-flowing, professional and really good – an intense and wonderful session that took fifteen minutes flat.

Once I was outside with Mum, who'd been waiting for an eternity in her Mini, I told her that I didn't think this profession was for me: hours and hours of nothing and then a quarter of an hour of sheer pleasure.

'I understand, but that's so like you, Vic. Rollercoasters are your thing. You need heady sensations or else you get bored. I'm sure that the further you go in this profession, the more really memorable moments you'll have.'

I wish I'd been as sure as she was.

As a result, at the next photo shoot – a page for the English magazine *Wonderland* for which I wore a sublime pair of Louboutins that I would very much have liked to take home with me – I really let myself have some fun. These instants in front of the photographer's lens are *the* moments to savour, and I had a ball. I laughed, I danced, I acted the madwoman; the more he encouraged me, the further I went, as if I were an actress who was completely in character. If this is what my life consisted of, then at least I should make the most of it.

I was still in that state of post-session excitement when Daniela, the Argentinian make-up artist who I'd had a good chat with while she was getting me ready, said to me a little shyly, 'You know, Victoire, I've got a little sister I adore. She's very beautiful, she's 16 and her dream is to become a model.'

'Oh no!' My reply shot out of my mouth before I had time to think what I was saying. I started explaining myself and then I just couldn't hold back. I described how difficult this profession was for young girls, how they got treated as objects and how they obsessed over eating and not putting on an ounce, without the issue ever being raised; I told her about the cynicism, the aggressiveness of the other girls, the competitiveness, the solitude, the endless hours spent waiting for so little in return. She couldn't get over what I was saying, because I looked so happy after my photo shoot! I couldn't believe either that I was expressing, so emphatically and with such conviction, things that I'd never formulated with such clarity before. It really was time that I thought about my future seriously.

When I got back home, I had a call from Flo: 'Victoire, are you sitting comfortably? You're returning to London on the weekend of 11 November. Miu Miu have chosen you to do their campaign!'

Mum and I arranged everything so that we could go together: three days in London, the two of us, in a nice hotel paid for by the client! During the day, while I was working, Mum could wander around the art galleries and then we'd spend the evenings together. Sometimes life as a clothes hanger was cool!

The first day was perfect: we got there in the afternoon, had a little stroll around the streets of London and then had dinner in our beautiful hotel room. I went to bed early without taking an enema – Mum didn't know about that and I could never have done it in her presence – in order to be on

top form the next day: the schedule Flo had sent me stipu-
lated that a chauffeur would pick me up at seven o'clock on
the dot and would bring me home at six o'clock. Mert and
Marcus, *the* star pair of photographers of the moment, would
be doing the photo shoot.

The next morning in the hotel lobby, I discovered that I
wasn't alone: two other models, a Dutch brunette and a
Russian blonde who seemed to be as surprised as I was, were
also waiting for the chauffeur. We got into the car without a
word and headed off to a warehouse in the suburbs.

As soon as I walked in, I could see that nothing was ready.
The technicians arrived at the same time as us and started
unrolling their cables and putting up the set, which was a
huge red-lacquered stage placed in front of an attractive
black wall. The studio manager confirmed that everything
would take at least two or three hours to set up and that
Mert and Marcus weren't due until early afternoon. When I
asked why, if that was the case, we'd been asked to come here
so early, she looked at me as if I had asked an incredibly
stupid question and just got on with what she was doing
without even bothering to reply.

The heat was absolutely stifling. I looked around the premises to pass the time. Downstairs the entire Miu Miu collection was waiting for us, carefully arranged on tables and
clothes racks. Next door was the make-up room with three
tables, three mirrors and three armchairs, and then upstairs
there was the hairstyling room, manned by a pleasant and
talkative hairstylist who I had a long chat with. When I

pushed open the door to the adjoining room, I discovered an amazing and terribly appetising buffet. My little voice instructed me not to touch it and to go straight back downstairs.

I got the first modules of the marketing course that the National Centre for Distance Education had sent me out of my bag: I'd figured that I might as well take advantage of all these hours spent waiting in order to learn a thing or two, but it was impossible. Since all the revision for Sciences Po, I was just no longer able to concentrate on a book, a newspaper or a lesson. I used to digest pages and pages of books of all kinds, and now I was reduced to reading the same paragraph five times without any of it sticking in my head. Fortunately I had my iPhone. Mum was sending me texts and photos of her day: a visit to the Tate Gallery, exhibitions in Mayfair, shopping in Carnaby Street ...

When Olivier arrived at around midday, I made a superhuman effort not to let him see how annoyed I was. 'Hello, Victoire! It's so nice to see you here! Everything OK?'

No, everything was not OK. I'd got up at six in the morning and had done nothing but wait in this rotten warehouse for those two bastard photographers to grace us with their presence and maybe to photograph me one of these days. But I took the more prudent option and answered with a smile.

The studio manager announced a lunch break – a break within a break before going back to the waiting – and we all gathered around that evil buffet. My two little comrades sensibly prepared themselves a bowl of muesli without sugar or fat or anything else, which they mixed with a sugar-free, fat-free yoghurt, while I went for a plate of breaded fish with French beans. Olivier sat down next to me to eat his steamed chicken and vegetables. I carefully removed the bread crust from my fish and pushed it to the edge of the plate.

'Don't you like breadcrumbs?'

'No, not really.'

After the meal, everyone returned to their posts. I went back up to the buffet to retrieve my plate, which I'd hidden in a corner, and ate the precious bread crust like it was a slice of cake – it was delicious. And since there was no one there watching me, I also got to taste the caramelised chicken brochettes which had been tempting me throughout the meal. I'd never eaten anything so tasty, so succulent or so divine, at least not for a long time.

Mert and Marcus finally arrived at around four o'clock. Everything was ready, but they decided to start with the Dutch girl. I went back upstairs to eat a couple of chicken brochettes while I was waiting my turn. When they'd finished with the brunette, they summoned the blonde and I returned to the buffet. Even cold, those brochettes were a knockout.

When my turn finally came, it was past eight o'clock and the brochettes had all been polished off. I got my make-up retouched, put on a dress – the same one I'd worn for the Palais-Royal show – and Olivier took me over to the stage to offer me up as a plaything to the gods of the camera. I didn't even want to do their bloody campaign any more, and here I was, plonked in the middle of the red stage while these two gentlemen, who didn't even say hello to me, talked to each other in low voices. One of them, I didn't know if it was Mert or Marcus because they hadn't introduced themselves, came over to me with his hand outstretched.

Ah, that was more like it! I held out my hand and said, 'Hello, I'm Victoire.'

But instead of taking my hand, he took my arm to move me over to the rattan chair placed next to me. 'Can you sit down please?' I wasn't sure if I was more embarrassed about having greeted somebody who clearly didn't give a damn about me, or more angry about being treated like shit by these two nonentities, for the pleasure of whose company I'd been waiting for twelve hours. Anyway, I sat down. 'Look to your left.' And I did. An assistant was pressing the button on the photographer duo's camera, which meant that they weren't even taking the photos themselves. He gestured to me to look right. Another click of the shutter. 'Stand up.' And I did. 'Look at me.' At which one? Him or him? 'OK, thank you.' And it was all over.

I'd been careful to count, and the assistant had pressed the button four times. So I'd been waiting twelve hours for four lousy shots? I came down off the stage and glanced at the assistant's computer screen: he was busy pasting my image next to the image of the other two. So why hadn't they got us all to pose together? God only knows. I noticed on the photos that I had a very stern look, much more so than the other two. I fretted about this to Olivier: they hadn't given me any instructions, but perhaps they would have preferred me to have had softer eyes? 'No, no, it's perfect like that. They want something strong, something different.'

It was nearly ten o'clock when I got back to the hotel. I collapsed in tears into Mum's arms; she'd been waiting for me since six as planned. I told her about the overheated warehouse, the day of waiting and the four lousy photos. I didn't say anything about the fish, the breadcrumbs or the brochettes – or about my anxiety over not being able to take an enema to get rid of it all. I said that I didn't want to be in this profession any more.

She was furious to see me in such a state and to learn that they could treat me in such a way. 'It's totally unacceptable. I'm going to call Florence!' My gentle pretty mother turned into a ferocious lion on the phone – it was almost scary. You didn't mess with her little ones.

I took a very hot bath, set the alarm for six o'clock to be ready for seven, swallowed a sleeping pill and a tranquilliser, and fell asleep in Mum's arms.

The next morning at seven I joined the girls in the hotel lobby. The chauffeur arrived and uttered a name. The Dutch girl said, 'Yes, that's me.' He gestured to her to follow him.

The Russian girl asked, 'What about me?'

The chauffeur said, 'No, just her.'

And off the two of them went.

I called Flo, who was gobsmacked. She called Russell and then called me back to tell me that Miu Miu would, it transpired, be doing their campaign with just the Dutch girl and that I could come back to Paris.

'But Mum and I have got Eurostar tickets for tomorrow. We can't exchange them.'

'Listen, Victoire, that's not my problem. Stay in London if you want to, but the client won't pay for the hotel tonight.'

We decided to return to Paris. Dad was apoplectic when he found out. He called Flo to demand an explanation. After they got off the phone, Flo's call to me lit the blue touchpaper: 'Victoire, I work with you, not with your parents. Either you manage to handle things yourself, or we'll have to reconsider your position.'

I had already reconsidered my position: I didn't want to be in this profession any more.

Weightless

I SIGNED UP FOR INTRODUCTORY classes at all the drama schools that offered them; it gave me the chance to spend a few hours observing at the Cours Galabru, the Cours Florent and the Studio Muller to find out what life as a budding actress might look like, and I liked what I saw. It was exciting and it was what I wanted to do.

During a stormy meeting with Flo, she slyly suggested entrusting me to Solène, who looked after the new faces. 'I wouldn't be offended, if that's what you prefer. She's more used to dealing with the parents and the anxieties of the novices than I am. You ask lots of questions, far too many. You want explanations. I haven't got time for all that.'

I was the one who felt offended, but I didn't say so. I wasn't stupid and I could see that if I agreed, I'd be demoted from the status of rising top model to that of novice model. It would be a crushing setback.

Once I got home, I had a long talk with Dad, who told me to keep my chin up and to soldier on. 'Sweetpea, you're not going to give up at the first sign of difficulty, are you?'

The first? With rare exceptions, these last few months had been nothing but pain and hardship. I knew Dad wanted the best for me, but he just didn't appreciate the situation. He didn't spend his days with me and so he didn't see or realise what was happening. Plus, he himself always saw things through, even when it was tough. Whether it was studying to get into college, his university studies or his job, when he started something he always finished it.

He insisted that I call Louis at Silent to see if he could find me that much touted campaign that would mark the start of my career.

Louis was adorable and comforting and consoling. 'Don't fret, Victoire, you've only been on the circuit for three months! Unfortunate things like this happen, but you're preparing the ground for a terrific future. Everybody has noticed you: Phillip Lim is interested in you, and you alone, for his lookbook and Calvin Klein have taken out an option to have exclusive rights to you in February. You're being talked about throughout the industry. I thought you wanted to take a bit of a breather, but if you're interested, we can organise a week of castings and photo shoots in New York at the beginning of December to really cement your presence.'

It seemed like a good idea to me, providing Mum could come with me; returning to New York on my own was out of the question.

'OK, I'll call you back. Until then, get some rest, Victoire. And stop worrying.'

I ran into Samuel Drira again at a Lacoste shoot and we had a lot of fun. We spent the day pretending to play sport in little striped white and navy blue outfits and trainers, caps and sunglasses. I tried on a size 8 tracksuit and it was much too big for me, despite the fact that I weighed 50 and a bit kilos. I scrutinised the figure I could see in the large changing room mirror: no cheeks, no breasts, no stomach and no buttocks. My thighs were distinctly separated from each other by a nice hollow thigh gap. That was me – that ultra-thin and ultra-determined girl, who was in perfect control of her body, her appetite, her weight and her life. And now I was going to ruin it all.

At lunch I ate with the crew and I had a bit of everything, just like they did. An assistant watched me polish off my plate with admiration: 'So it's true, then? There really are girls who can eat normally without putting on an ounce. Do you realise how lucky you are, Victoire?' Oh, shut up.

Things really started picking up on 26 November. Flo left a message to say that a Turkish magazine had booked me for a photo shoot in Wales. 'You leave tomorrow and you come back on the 29th, just in time to take the plane to New York.' I just didn't want to go – I didn't give a toss about the Turks, their magazine or Wales and I was going to stay at home. Mum took care of the phone call to Flo to break the news; it was the first time I'd said no. 'You must understand, Florence, she's really very tired. She needs to rest.'

Flo must have been furious, but that was too bad. On the 27th, there was another message: 'Victoire, great news!

You're off to Miami for a shoot with the Australian photographer Benny Horne for Fendi and another one into the bargain for the magazine *Wonderland*. I've arranged things with Silent: I'll take care of the Miami–New York leg so that you're there on 1st December as planned.'

I burst into tears in front of a disconsolate Alex, who had just got home and who couldn't understand: 'You're crying because you're being "forced" to go to Miami?'

Before packing my bags, I called Sophie to cancel our Paris meet-up for the umpteenth time. 'Sophie, I'm sorry, but I can't make it tomorrow after all.'

'Are you taking the piss?'

'No, I'm off to Miami.'

'OK, have a nice trip.' And she hung up on me.

That evening, Léo came and lay down in bed with me. 'Don't worry, Vic, you'll get through it.'

I told him that although Mum and Dad didn't know it yet, I'd decided to quit this shitty profession which was driving me up the wall and which, more than anything, was making me more and more brain-dead.

'I find that hard to believe. You know perfectly well that you're not remotely brain-dead.'

Through my sobs, I explained to him that I'd just lost my best friend, that I wasn't even capable of reading a newspaper any more, that I was afraid all the time of everything and that I was fed up of feeling hungry, of being alone and of people expecting me to behave like an adult and then treating me like a child, like a piece of shit, like a clothes hanger.

'You're not a clothes hanger, Vic. You're the most beautiful girl in the world. And whatever you decide to do, we'll always love you to bits.'

And so off I went to Miami on my own, with just Yùki for company. The chauffeur wasn't there when I arrived. I called the number Louis had given me and yelled down the phone like a madwoman. He turned up all contrite half an hour later, apologising profusely, and I behaved hatefully towards him. I jumped into his hicksville car with its leopard-skin seats and teddy bear collection on the back shelf and heaped contempt on him. The more he apologised, the more I did him down.

I eventually calmed down at the sight of the palm trees through the window and the yachts, the dream villas and the huge hotels lining the beach. It was summer in the middle of winter. The weather was splendid and I was a little 18-year-old girl who thought she had the right to put this poor man, who could have been my father, through the wringer just because he'd kept me waiting for half an hour before taking me to a superb hotel which was being paid for by the client. I felt ashamed. I was in the process of becoming a bitch, just like the other girls.

I apologised, he said it was 'OK' and then he dropped me off at an amazing hotel like the ones you see in the films: a wonder of colonial architecture with its white wood, tropical flowers, palm trees, array of terraces and staircases that led down directly to a sublime sandy beach. In the indoor garden, which was as lush as a jungle, there were white birdcages full of multicoloured birds.

My bedroom was huge, with a large four-poster bed and a balcony from which I could observe a parade of immaculately tanned swimmers and nymphs with perfect boob jobs.

The photo crew welcomed me like a princess. The dresser took me into the suite, which they had turned into a changing room, to show me her treasures: Dior, Chanel, Versace and Emilio Pucci dresses which were more beautiful than any I'd ever seen. We got to know each other while sharing a fabulous buffet from which I picked out some wonderfully fresh and exotic fruit, and then I went off to bed, completely shattered from the jet-lag and all the emotion of recent days.

'Sleep well, Victoire! See you at four tomorrow morning on the beach, just before sunrise, to do some photos in the dawn light.'

It was too hot to sleep. I went downstairs and settled myself in a deckchair by the softly lit emerald-green pool. I was feeling in a really bad way, jet-lagged and lost. Here I was in one of the most beautiful places in the world, and I just didn't exist. I was devoid of feelings and thoughts.

It was as if I were dead.

I called home and Alexis picked up. I described what I could see from where I was sitting and he replied, 'Wow – that's just amazing! Can you imagine, it's snowing here!' No, I couldn't imagine. It was like I was weightless. I couldn't picture in my mind that I was here in summer and they were over there in winter. I hung up and went for a walk on the beach with my feet in the water, just like I used to in La Baule. I thought of Granddaddy, of the boys and Mum and Dad, of

Sophie who didn't want to see me again, and of my life before, when everything had been so much simpler.

I went back up to bed and took an enema to eliminate all that fruit. I sent a photo of my room to Mum, who responded with a: 'Wow! How lucky you are! Amazing!' And then I curled up in my huge four-poster bed and went to sleep, hugging Yùki tightly and completely on my own.

The alarm clock went off at half past three. I took a quick shower to wake myself up, drank a large glass of water and headed down to the beach. They were all already there; there was a table and a chair set out under a parasol for doing my make-up and hair and those sublime dresses were hanging on a rack and floating in the night-time breeze. There were croissants and fruit on another table as well as hot and cold drinks. In the light from a projector, they styled my hair and applied some light make-up. Standing barefoot in the almost lukewarm water, I put on my first dress, which was a silk one. The glow of dawn was turning the horizon red. Benny Horne, the photographer, asked me in a very gentle voice, so as not to spoil this magical moment, to walk into the water in my dress. 'Do what you think feels right.' I'm not too sure what I did – I was there but elsewhere at the same time, as if I'd dissolved and was outside time among these adorable people on a paradise beach at sunrise. I changed dresses and a bright red sun appeared on the horizon. I had the impression that I could have taken it in my arms. I danced and floated in and on the water and in the wind, this way, that way, my arms and legs and hair and hips all in motion. My body was so light that I couldn't feel it any more and so empty that it could almost have floated away.

I let the gentle waves lap around me and take me where they wanted, thinking to myself, If I float, so much the better. If I sink, too bad. Wrapped in silk and swayed by the sea, nothing else mattered or was even real.

Benny seemed enchanted: 'You are so marvellous, Victoire! Unbelievable!'

By the time we were done, it was broad daylight and actually starting to get very hot. They all got undressed and we laughed and swam in this extraordinary place where we'd all just had an equally extraordinary experience, and then we went back to the hotel for lunch.

Even after showering, oiling my skin and getting dressed, I was still rather intoxicated by this very special experience. Drunk, even, on all the weeks that had led up to this point, on the floods of tears I'd endured and on the endless fasting that had exhausted my body and my brain. Now I'd thrown everything overboard: my fears, my anxieties, my desires and my fits of anger, and even the bastard voice had shut up for once. There was nothing left of me but this virtually empty body which they all found so 'perfect' and an irrepressible urge to laugh at the slightest thing, as if I'd smoked an enormous joint. We met up in the hotel restaurant and I tucked into a delicious mahi-mahi which was perfectly marinated in … Well, who cared what it was marinated in.

Then we set off in a pink caravan, which looked like it belonged to Barbie and was fitted out as a make-up studio, and they spent the afternoon photographing me in Fendi dresses in a gallery full of contemporary artworks. I began to feel increasingly out of it, I couldn't stop laughing and I was feeling shakier and shakier on my feet. Benny encouraged me to keep going until he had what he wanted. 'Victoire, do you want us to get you something to eat?' I didn't want to eat – I'd already eaten more than enough. I was feeling ever more fragile and insubstantial, as if I were in the process of disappearing altogether. We did one last series and then they took me back to the hotel before heading off to get the last plane home. My plane was leaving the following morning. We all hugged each other as if we'd known each other for ever and loved each other like mad. And that was exactly how I felt: they were like a little family who I loved very much and who I'd shared one of those incredible moments with that I would never ever forget.

But that family was disappearing as suddenly as it had appeared; they left and I collapsed on my king-size bed, all alone.

The Bitch

I WAS STILL OUT OF IT the following day when I took the plane to New York. But I was no longer alone – the little voice had returned and was on top form. It had completely taken over my mind, my body and my thoughts. Its refrain was still the same: 'You're too fat. Stop eating. You're too fat.' And it was right: I had to stop eating.

I arrived at the hotel that Silent had booked me into in Times Square. I had a small suite on the fifth floor, which you accessed with an electronic card. There was a big mirrored bathroom, a pointless kitchen area and an attractive bedroom with a large bay window looking out onto the city. I unpacked, put my scales in the bathroom and got undressed. The mirrors reflected the image of my enormous body: fat around my stomach, fat on my arms and fat on my buttocks. I weighed myself: 49 kilos. I would stop eating until I got back down to 47. And to speed things up, I'd do all my travelling on foot. Sport was forbidden, but walking was allowed. In any case, Mum wasn't there yet and so I had nothing better to do than to walk from one appointment to the next until she arrived.

Louis had sent me a schedule: I had meetings with some big-name fashion photographers so that they could get to know me, have a look at my book and get a sense of my personality. They would then hopefully think of me the next time a magazine commissioned a shoot from them. 'All you have to do is turn up with your book and your comp cards and be yourself.' I showered, put on my skinny trousers and my model's high heels, wrapped myself up in my big puffa jacket to ward off the late autumn cold and headed out once again to conquer New York.

I walked for miles on end, taking big strides to keep me warm and to lose my excess fat. The photographers I met greeted me with a certain indifference. 'There's not an awful lot in your book.' Well no, I'm just starting out. That's why I'm here. There were sweet ones and mad ones, healthy types and drugged-out guys. It was back to the spectacle of the assistants dancing to the tune of their masters and clicking the shutter for them like with Mert and Marcus. I really suffered from the cold. When I couldn't put up with it any longer, I'd stop off at a Starbucks and drink a large and disgusting coffee, heavily watered down. 'You're too fat. Stop eating. You're too fat.' I also gave up the chewing gum and the Pepsi Max to lose weight more quickly. I couldn't see New York any more or the people or anything else. I was simply alone, with my bastard little voice, striding around the city to lose my fat.

* * *

Mum arrived on 3 December at around three o'clock. I had appointments that whole afternoon. I'd let the hotel doorman know that she'd be coming to see him for the electronic card to get into my room. When I got out of my meetings at about five, I found my voicemail full of messages from Mum: he hadn't allowed her up to my room and she was waiting for me in the hotel foyer. I virtually ran back to the hotel in an unspeakable rage. I arrived at the hotel like a vengeful goddess and made a beeline for the doorman, with murder in mind. I bawled him out, telling him he was an incompetent, an idiot and a halfwit, that he didn't have to be a genius to give the card to a woman who had the same name as me, that I had reminded him about it that very morning and that it was his job to follow instructions.

Mum, whom I hadn't even said hello to, came over and told me to calm down. No, I wouldn't calm down, I couldn't believe how inept the guy was and I was going to write to the hotel management to get him fired! He was completely at a loss and kept on saying, 'Sorry, miss, sorry,' like an automaton. Mum was horrified and kept saying sorry too, but to him, as she tried to usher me towards the lift.

When we got to my room, I opened the bedroom door, went over to the bay window and said, 'If there wasn't any glass, I could fly away.' I felt hollow now, as if my anger had completely emptied me of all emotion. Mum began to cry. 'Loutch, you're in a really bad way.' I lay down on the bed. I wasn't in a bad way. In fact, I felt just fine, because I couldn't feel anything any more.

What I needed was a bath.

And so I went into the bathroom and while the tub was filling up, I conducted another inspection: fat around the stomach, fat on the arms, fat on the buttocks and 48.4. Mum knocked on the door and I told her to come in.

She opened the door and I saw her eyes in the mirror, looking me up and down. Then she collapsed sobbing to the floor. 'Just look at yourself, Victoire! You look like you've just got out of a concentration camp!' She couldn't see that I was huge. I showed her the fat all over me. She couldn't stop crying. 'You have to stop this, you're killing yourself.'

I couldn't understand what she was talking about.

She got up, came over and took me in her arms. I recoiled – I didn't want to be touched by anyone, not even by her. I didn't want to be touched by anyone any more, I didn't have a body any more.

I wasn't real any more. I just wanted to vanish so that it would all be over.

I think I fell asleep. At one point, I heard her talking to Dad: 'We're going to come home, it's out of hand. She has to stop. It's too dangerous for her.'

I said no: I was here for my appointments, and I'd go to my appointments.

When I woke up the next morning, I felt extremely hungry. When I said so to Mum, she offered me some fruit, but I didn't want to eat fruit – I wanted some proper food. 'How about some chicken? Do you want me to go and get you some chicken?' And so she went down to find me some chicken.

The wait was unbearable and all the time the little voice was saying, 'Stop eating,' while my stomach was saying, 'Eat, eat, you're hungry.' When she got back with a whole roast chicken, I pounced on it and ate it with my hands, stuffing it into my mouth and devouring it down to the bones to satiate my hunger, to fill the void inside me, to soothe my pain and to silence the little voice.

It didn't work for long. The voice started screaming again: 'You're too fat. Stop eating. You're too fat.' I went into the bathroom and weighed myself: 48.5. I looked for the enema tube in my sponge bag.

Mum appeared and started crying again:

'Victoire, what are you doing?' She took the enema tube and threw it in the bin. I went and got it back out of the bin. She took it off me again. We almost got into a fight. She kept on saying, 'Stop it, stop it, stop it.'

She managed to get me onto the bed, and both of us cried together for a long time. And then I stopped crying, for good. I got up to get ready for my appointments. 'Victoire, we're going home.'

No way, I said. I'm here for my appointments, and I'm going to go to my appointments. She said she thought I should give up this profession. I felt the rage and the hatred welling up inside me again. I looked her straight in the eyes. 'Do you remember in Milan when I called you to say that I was going to quit? You said to me, "Don't quit, I'm on my

way." So there you go, and now it's too late. You wanted me
to carry on, and I'm carrying on. I signed up for a year. And
a year is what I'm going to do.'

I had become the little voice. Now I was the bitch.

I went to my appointments, one after another, like a robot. I
had the following afternoon off and so we went to see the
Frick Collection opposite Central Park on foot. It was bitterly
cold when we came out afterwards and Mum was shivering.
She wanted to take a cab back, but I said no – we would
walk. 'Victoire, don't speak to me in that tone of voice. I'm
freezing cold and exhausted. Let's get a cab back.' I refused
categorically. I had to walk in order to lose all this fat. If she
couldn't understand that, that was her problem. She started
crying, but I didn't give a damn. We returned on foot.

The following night, when she thought I was sleeping, I
heard her speaking to Dad. 'You should have seen her, as thin
as a rake, crouching in front of the window, her hair all over
the place, devouring the whole chicken right down to the
bones. She looked like a feral child.' I heard her, and yet I
didn't hear her. I was there, but it wasn't me. Only the worst
of me was left, all that was really bad in me. Hatred. Rage.
Fat. Death.

I no longer existed.

On 6 December I had an appointment with dear Phillip Lim
to model for his lookbook. Mum came with me and he
greeted us in his customary kindly way. I asked if Mum could

stay with us. 'Of course you can, please make yourself at home.' Once again I thought of that idiot Seb, who'd claimed you weren't allowed to turn up with your mother. He introduced us to the photographer, KT Auleta. She was a big name in the profession and yet she was just as friendly and uncomplicated as he was. The *Vogue USA* team were also there to do a feature on him, as he was one of the rising stars of the fashion world. 'This is Victoire, my special favourite model.' I adored this man.

For the lookbook, there were just the four of us: the photographer, Phillip, Mum and me. When he wasn't quite sure, he asked her for her opinion, which delighted her, and he was delighted too. For lunch he ordered some Thai food to introduce us to the cuisine of his native country. We went into an office and ate – well, they ate, I didn't – around a large table while we chatted. He told me a bit about his life and his career as a designer. It was a pleasant interlude, free of tension and with nothing on the line.

As we left, he hugged me. 'Thank you for everything, Victoire. We'll see each other in February for the show.'

We jumped in a taxi back to the hotel, packed our bags and went home to Paris.

I Quit

THE JOURNEY HOME WAS DREADFUL. Once again I reduced Mum to tears several times. I wasn't doing it on purpose, but I couldn't help myself. I said what was on my mind and it just came out, uncensored.

It was as if I were no longer me, and in fact I wasn't me any more. I wasn't even that bastard voice – I wasn't anybody at all any more, and it was somehow so very soothing ...

When we got home, I immediately shut myself in my bedroom – I didn't want to see anyone, not even the boys. I just wanted to be on my own with Plume and to be left in peace.

The next day my parents were waiting for me in the living room. I told them I'd honour the photo shoots planned for that month and then my mind was made up: I was quitting this profession.

Mum sighed: 'Yes, Loutch, you're right. You should quit.'

I looked at Dad and it seemed that he didn't agree. 'Victoire, you've signed a one-year contract. When you make a commitment, you stick to it. As soon as you get a campaign, everything will take off. Don't clip your wings before you get that far, Sweetpea.'

If only they could have made up their minds, it might have helped me to make up my own mind.

On 9 December I had an appointment with the photographer, his assistant, Céleste and Yohji Yamamoto's team at a caravan under I forget which bridge in Paris. Céleste and I quickly realised that the day was going to be a trying one. It was bitterly cold, the clothes to be presented were in fact items of underwear, accompanied by nothing but some little capes and some light tulle petticoats, and the photographer and his assistant were evidently more preoccupied with their love affair than they were with our presence.

And so there we were half-naked under the bridge waiting for these two little lovebirds, wrapped up in their puffa jackets, gloves and scarves, to find a moment amid all their billing and cooing to take a photo or two of us occasionally.

Glancing at their computer screen as I went off to change outfits, I noticed that they were erasing all the images in which you could see our faces, meaning that we'd been spending hours getting frozen for photos in which we couldn't even be identified! I felt the anger welling up inside me. Céleste tried to calm me down and reassure me: 'You know, he's a great photographer. One of the best.' But did that give him the right to treat us so badly and to dispense with our faces?

At lunchtime, meals were delivered to the lovers, but there was nothing for us. Still, everybody knew that models didn't eat.

Things got under way again after a 'nice hot coffee'. Virtually naked, we went back out in front of the lens of these sadistic lovers, who took all the time in the world to unleash their creativity. By the time we got to the final series, I couldn't bear it any more. We had been waiting for too long and I thought I was going catch my death of cold. I absolutely had to get warm and so I headed off in the direction of the caravan. The idiot photographer couldn't believe his eyes. 'But Victoire, what are you doing?' I replied that I was going to go and sit in the warm until he got himself ready and I slammed the door behind me to avoid any arguments.

We did the last photos and then they let us know that they couldn't take us home and that we'd have to take the metro. I was walking down into the station when my phone rang – it was Flo.

'What happened with the photographer, Victoire? He called me to say that you were rude to him.'

I replied that I'd merely spoken to him in the same way that he and his bitch of an assistant had spoken to me and that I'd gone back into the caravan to avoid freezing to death.

'But who do you think you are? He's one of the best in the profession! He takes sublime photos.'

I told her that I'd seen his photos and that there wasn't a single one in which you could actually recognise us.

'You know nothing about fashion, Victoire. He's the professional, not you. And if you don't like it, then all you have to do is quit.'

And I replied, 'You're right, Flo. I quit.' And I hung up.

So that was it – I'd done it. I was free at last.

As I was coming out of the metro, she called again. 'Listen, my dear. It's not a big deal. You're knackered, you've just got back from New York, you got a bit cross and we said things we didn't really mean.'

'No, I did mean it, Flo. This profession really pisses me off. I'll do tomorrow's shoot and the Céline lookbook as planned, and then I'm quitting.'

'Victoire, don't get carried away. I've got nothing but good news for you. I got the photos from Miami and you look wonderful! The photographer adored you!'

'Just now it was "who do you think you are?" and now suddenly I'm "wonderful"? This industry really makes me want to throw up.'

'You know, the annual rankings have just come out: you're one of the top twenty models of the year, which means you're booked up to the hilt. Everyone's calling to book you for the February shows. And Mario Testino, one of the photographers you met in New York last week and who works with *Vogue* regularly, is telling everyone that you really caught his eye.'

'I don't care, Flo. I've had enough.'

'Listen, go home and talk to your parents about it.'

Well, well, suddenly it *was* my parents' business. But it was too late now and in any case, since I'd told Dad I was quitting, he wasn't talking to me.

'Think about it, Victoire, and call me back.'

I had thought about it and she'd just have to get used to the idea.

The next day I had my final shoot for *Grey Magazine*, an Italian magazine that was so hip that nobody had ever heard of it. Mum came along with me. 'You can sit down there.'

'But Victoire, shouldn't you ask if they mind if I stay?'

'No.'

The photographer came and said hello and I didn't reply. The designer, a very young Italian who looked barely 15, came over in his turn to greet me. 'Hello, Victoire, how are you?'

'Listen, can we start? I'm tired.' This had an immediate effect: the more hateful I was, the more they catered to my every little need. It was just what I'd always suspected: I'd observed this phenomenon a hundred times over the last few months, and this time it was my turn to act like that.

Very rapidly, the designer began to panic and to lose it completely. I was given badly ironed clothes to put on, which he touched up with a steam iron when I already had them on. 'What do you think you're doing? Are you an idiot, or what?'

'Sorry, Victoire, sorry.'

'Just mind what you're doing rather than apologising!'

After a while, a disgusted Mum told me to start behaving properly.

'It's not my fault. The guy's a complete idiot!'

Unfortunately the photographer was even more inept than the designer. His slowness was incredibly exasperating – why did they all spend so much time examining their navels as if they were about to take the photo of the century? He got me to pose seated on the arm of a seventies chair and spent an age getting the focus right. 'Are you OK, Victoire, not too uncomfortable?'

Not at all, you wanker – I've got the arm of an iron chair up my arse and I'm loving it. He carried on with his adjustments while the iron bar cut into my buttocks. When it started hurting too much, I just stood up.

'Oh no, stay seated.'

'No, I'm not going to stay seated, my bum hurts. When you're done with your adjustments, I'll sit down and we can get to work.'

The whole thing was never-ending. Every time they asked me to do something, I replied insolently. I was well aware that it was unacceptable, but I wasn't in control of anything any more. When he clicked his fingers for the umpteenth time to summon his assistant, I yelled, 'Florian, for fuck's sake, his name is Florian!' Whereupon Mum got up and left.

When I joined her in the car an hour later, she was still furious. 'You were hateful, Victoire. You can't behave towards people like that. It's totally unacceptable.'

'Oh yeah? And how do you think they've all been behaving towards me these last few months?'

'We didn't bring you up like that. I don't recognise the person you've become.'

The rest of the journey home passed in silence and as soon as we arrived I went and shut myself in my room.

Everybody was pissing me off.

* * *

When Flo called the next day, I thought it would be to have a go at me because the photographer had complained, but on the contrary: 'Victoire, guess what? I've just had Samuel Drira on the phone and you've been chosen for the Lacoste campaign!'

'You don't understand, Flo, I'm quitting.'

'But surely you're not going to say no to Samuel Drira? You adore him!'

I hung up to avoid getting cross, grabbed my bag and went out for a walk and some fresh air.

I passed in front of a bakery and saw a sign in the window saying: 'House speciality: Nutella pizza'. That was exactly what I needed. I bought some *pains au chocolat*, some brioche and some Nutella pizzas – I was fully stocked up. The baker winked at me: 'Well, you've certainly got an appetite!'

'It's for the children I'm looking after – I'm on my way to pick them up from school.'

'What a cool babysitter they've got!'

I couldn't take all that back home, so I ate while I walked through the streets. I ate the lot, until I felt thoroughly sick, and then went home to take an enema.

Dad got home from work and told me Flo had called him about the Lacoste campaign. He said, 'It's done! You've got your campaign. It's brilliant news!'

I told him that I wasn't going to do it. He started to argue and I went and shut myself in my room.

The following day I found another bakery that sold big loaves of brioche. They were really huge and also soft, moist and delicious. And in the afternoon, I went back to the Nutella pizza place to get some more pizzas.

Flo kept calling me, but I didn't pick up. Then she texted me: 'You haven't forgotten about the Céline lookbook on 16 December?'

And I replied: 'No, I'll be there.'

At home I wasn't on speaking terms with anyone except for Plume, who was always ready to listen to me. I also spoke a bit to Léo, who didn't seem to understand his big sister at all any more. I didn't understand anything either. Everything was beyond my control. And I just ate and ate and ate. The laxatives were no longer working at all and the enemas were becoming less effective.

On 16 December I weighed myself before heading off to see Phoebe Philo to do her lookbook: 54 kilos. I'd never get into the clothes. Perhaps into the size 8 at a squeeze, but definitely not into the size 6. I went there like a fat cow to the slaughter. When I greeted Phoebe, I wanted to die. Suzie was there, as thin as ever and still not being selected for the shows. Then it was into the make-up, hair and hanging around routine.

I tried on the first pair of trousers and I managed to button them up, but only just. The photographer began by photographing me face on, in profile and in three-quarter profile. This guy didn't know what he wanted. Phoebe was watching me impassively without saying a word. The photographer thanked me and signalled to Suzie. I went back to the dressing room, took off that tight pair of trousers and waited for somebody to show me my next outfit, but nobody said anything to me for a very long time. I saw Suzie getting changed, going off and coming back, and getting changed once again. I waited for my turn, which never came.

I started to get bored and prowled around the buffet. There was a mountain of croissants and other sweet pastries. The bastard little voice struck up its refrain again but I told it to shut it. If they didn't want me, I was going to eat, and that was their problem. In any case, I'd finally got to the point where I couldn't get into the clothes. I hadn't had a brain for a long time, but now I didn't even have a body.

They never called me again. I spent the day waiting and eating, and then I went home.

I stayed in bed for several days on end. I only got up to go to the chemist for some laxatives, enemas and tranquillisers. I covered all the chemists in the area, one after the other, serving up my spiel to them. I covered all the bakeries and the delicatessens too, buying cakes that I hid under my bed.

We spent Christmas as a family, but I have hardly any recollection of it, except that I ate incessantly.

By the morning of 29 December, I'd reached 58 kilos and so I was back to where I'd started. Flo hadn't rung me in days. When I saw her name come up on my phone, I didn't answer – I was terrified. But she was persistent and eventually I picked up. 'Victoire, my dear, you'll never guess! I've just got the confirmation that you've been chosen for the cover of *Vogue Italia*.'

'Flo, it's no. I've told you, it's finished. I'm quitting.' I hung up.

Even if I changed my mind, who would still want me? I'd become enormous, monstrous, unshowable.

Disappearing

I WEIGHED MYSELF this morning and I was 64 kilos. I
didn't even know why I was still weighing myself. I'd had the
perfect body and I'd ruined it like everything else, including
my friendships and my relationship with my parents, who I
hadn't spoken to for days except to listen to them telling me
that I was eating too much, as if I didn't know that already.
I'd failed the Sciences Po exam too and I had no plans and no
future. Even acting was screwed.

I was screwed.

The previous month, Seb had called: 'Victoire, sweetheart!
Everybody wants you for February.' Go to hell, Seb.

Flo didn't give up and rolled off a list of names to me:
Russell Marsh, Calvin Klein, Phillip Lim, Samuel Drira etc.
Apparently she was just refusing to listen. I should have told
her that it was dead in the water, that I was now a size 10 –
that would soon have quietened her down.

The previous week my cousin Thomas had become persistent too: he wanted me to go to the cinema with him. He'd
been coming to see me regularly and was trying to persuade
me that I was 'much better off like this. You were terribly

thin, Victoire.' Nan said the same thing to me, but she loved me so much that she'd have said anything to make me feel better. I ended up giving in to Tom and spent an hour finding an outfit I could still get into. I bumped into Mum in the hall and she jumped: 'I didn't recognise you! I've got to get used to you having cheeks again.'

I went back up to my room and texted Thomas – I couldn't show myself like that in public.

The only time I forced myself to go out was when I accompanied Granddaddy to the Pompidou Centre, disguised in a long coat and a big black hat. As we were coming out of the exhibition, I heard somebody calling out to me by my first name: it was Daniel Peddle, a New York casting director. 'I saw you from the back and I knew straight away that you were a model.' An ex-model. He listed all the shows I was already booked for in February and the requests for options that kept flooding in. I told him that I wouldn't be at the next fashion week because I was resuming my studies. He seemed to be genuinely disappointed, but also happy for me.

Sophie never called me back and I didn't dare chase her up. I could understand her disgust, because she'd been so patient with me. And what would I have said to her if I had rung her? I had nothing else to say.

Alex was still getting me to listen to music and Puggy's album was on a loop in my ears:

Safe from them all
Those evil little motherfuckers at my door
Yeah, well I've kept score
And I believe they owe me more than life is
Short

So I will stay with you
I will stay with you
I will stay with you
How I needed you

Rather than expressing his feelings by telling me directly how he felt, Alex was getting Puggy to do it for him.

I thought back to his moist eyes at San Francisco airport just before he said to me: 'Sis, you're the most beautiful girl. And I love you.' He had the same eyes now when he looked at me. As for my little Léo, he often came into my room to talk to me. At the grand old age of 12, he listened to me and tried to find the right words: 'But Vic, you'll always be the most beautiful of them all! Don't worry, things are going to be fine.'

I wasn't worried, Léo, but no, things weren't going to be fine. The suffering had become unbearable, as had that bastard little voice, which was repeating incessantly: 'You're fat, you're ugly, you're crap. You screwed everything up. Eat, eat! That's the only thing you're good at.' I wanted to rest, to get out of this unspeakable, hateful world. I wanted it all to stop.

I wanted it all to stop.

I went round the house collecting up all the boxes of pills, got a large glass of water from the kitchen and got back into bed between Plume and Yùki. I emptied all the pills out into my hand and then I swallowed them. All the way down.

Léo came into my room as if through a fog.

He said, 'Vic, what are you doing?'

And I replied, 'Don't worry, my darling.'

And then everything did stop.

Not Alone Any More

I WOKE UP IN A HOSPITAL BED with a terrible urge to vomit. Everything around me was white and blurred and the place smelled of medicine.

So I'd screwed that up too. Mum and Dad came into my room accompanied by a guy in a white coat. They looked lost, sad and determined all at the same time – determined to act and to take things in hand.

The doctor began to explain to them in a professional tone and using incomprehensible jargon what was happening to my body and to me, as if I wasn't there and didn't exist.

So here we go again.

My hatred of everything poured forth. I snarled like a rabid dog at this guy who couldn't even be bothered to speak intelligibly and directly to me. In the midst of my fog, I heard him say condescendingly, 'OK, she's doing her teenager crisis routine.' Wanker.

I adopted a calmer tone and told him that, on the contrary, everything was absolutely fine. 'It was all just a mistake. I want to go home.'

Mum looked at me sternly and told me in no uncertain terms to stop pretending. 'No, you're not fine, Victoire. You're not fine at all.'

God, they were pissing me off with all this wanting to save me! It was my life and I would do what *I* wanted to do.

As soon as they'd sorted out the formalities, I called Sophie: it was an SOS. I knew that she'd always be there for me. I begged her to call my mother and tell her to get me out of there.

'Don't worry, Vic, I'll take care of it. Just you hang on in there …'

By the end of the afternoon, I was still writhing angrily in my hospital bed and feeling nauseous. Mum and Dad finally came to pick me up. 'We're taking you out of here, Loutch, and we're going to help you. We've found just the right place for you.'

I didn't try to argue and off we went. I don't remember the journey, except that there were the three of us in the car and I was fighting against the urge to vomit and to sleep. I wasn't even angry any more – I wasn't anything any more. My eyes were flickering open and shut and I could hear snippets of what Mum was saying: 'She mustn't find herself in an ugly, depressing clinic. The environment counts for a lot … She's got to have activities to keep her busy all the time.' Dad didn't say a word and neither did I. I think we were all completely overwhelmed by the situation.

* * *

When we came to a halt outside what looked like a council block, Mum checked the address twice before declaring that leaving me here was out of the question. Dad started to get cross but she'd already gone into the clinic to retrieve my patient records, which the Sainte-Anne psychiatric hospital had sent them a few hours earlier. When she came back, she had her phone to her ear and proceeded to tap a new address into the satnav: Garches, on the western outskirts of Paris.

We passed through a large black gate into an attractive estate which felt like it was in the middle of the countryside. There was a gravel avenue lined with trees and small huddles of people in the grounds. At the end of the avenue, there was a massive white house, a palace virtually. Mum told me that this was where Antoine de Saint-Exupéry had written *The Little Prince*. Dad parked the car, they helped me out and then hugged me tightly against them while we walked up to the door of the annexe adjoining the house. We rang the bell and the door opened onto a welcoming hall which led to a library. It smelled of wax and fireplaces – you'd have thought it was a family home.

A tall blond-haired man with very blue eyes came towards us with a smile on his face. He held out his hand: 'Victoire, I presume? I'm Dr Vincent Jost. Nice to meet you. Would you like your parents to come with us or would you prefer to come with me on your own?'

I didn't know the answer to anything any more. It had been such a long time since I'd last made a decision for myself.

All of us sat down opposite him in his office. 'So tell me, what has brought you here?'

I lowered my eyes and started to cry. Mum took my hand and squeezed it very tightly. She started to speak and then Dad filled in the details. I looked at him and as I listened, I realised that he'd understood.

I wasn't alone any more.

Dr Jost asked my parents to wait for us in the library. He told me that I would be staying here for three months, if that was OK with me, that I would have time to myself, that we'd see each other every day, that I could do some acting, some yoga, some sport and some art therapy, that I'd decide how often my family came to see me and that I'd feel at home here and safe. He was funny, sensitive, intelligent and delicate. He spoke to me as an equal, and yes, of course I was OK with it.

When I came out of his room, Mum smiled at me: 'It's such a long time since we last heard you laugh.' They had found the right place and the right doctor and I was finally going to be able to let go.

The director of the establishment came to get us to escort us to the far side of the grounds. Mum took my hand and on the way we saw two terribly thin young women who were being reprimanded by a nurse for running around. We arrived at an outbuilding that contained quite a number of small bedrooms. There was a man in his fifties sitting at one of the tables on the terrace who looked absolutely exhausted. No doubt he was shot full of drugs and completely out of it.

These people were like me, and I was like them. I fitted into this environment and I felt good, at last. At the top of the steps, Dad took me in his arms and hugged me very tightly. 'You're going to get better, my love.'

That was the moment when I knew that I was saved.

It's a Wonderful Life

I SPENT THREE RESTFUL and wholesome months at the clinic. The medical examination revealed the sheer extent of the damage: amenorrhoea, hypotension, a good deal of hair loss and the skeleton of a 70-year-old woman.

I took an unconscionable number of calcium pills every day, I devised my diet with my nutritionist and I talked – an awful lot. I drew and I cried and I danced in the rain, and little by little I got back on my feet.

It was as if I were retrieving my true self.

I looked at the photos and videos from my season in fashion. There was me and the others with our thin bodies and our eyes shining brightly from lack of food – ghostlike figures in our sophisticated make-up. It was a parade of dark-ringed eyes set against porcelain skin.

I wrote short notes to the people I'd enjoyed meeting in order to thank them and to tell them that I'd decided to resume my studies. Phillip Lim replied: 'I'm so sad, but also so proud of you. It was a real honour to work with you. If more girls were like you, the industry would be a much better place ... Please do stay in touch, I'll miss you. Come to New York whenever you like ...'

Bouba replied too: 'Dear Victoire, you're very definitely not like all the other girls, and so much the better. Fill your already well-stocked head – you've made the right choice.'

And Louis and Émile: 'That doesn't surprise us, you asked far too many questions! In this profession, yours is not to reason why ...'

And, of course, my dear Russell Marsh: 'Victoire, I knew you weren't like the others and that you would give it up. That's the whole difficulty of my profession: in this industry, you try to nurture elite models and then the following season, they want new girls. And when you meet one and you think, that one's going to have a long career, she leaves. So what am I supposed to do?'

I kept their precious messages like little treasures to remind me that I really had experienced all that.

At the end of May, a few weeks after I came out of the clinic, Flo called to say that 'everyone was waiting for me' in New York in September. I told her that I weighed 69 kilos. She replied: 'That's not a problem. September's three months away.' I hung up, for the very last time.

My contracts expired in July and I received the final accounts, or rather the final list of deductions – that was when I realised what they really meant by 'we advance your expenses'. All Seb's taxis were on me. And the hairdresser, the smelly khaki jacket and the photo session with Sergei. And the walking

lessons with Évelyne and the plane tickets. And the chauffeur-driven cars, Riccardo's waiting time in Milan, the phone
calls in all the countries, the hotels and the fruit platters. Even
the printing of the books and comp cards. And then I found
out that, with the exception of Céline and Vanessa Bruno, all
those 'gifts' from the designers where they invited us to
choose 'for free' from their stock at the end of the shows
weren't gifts at all but a one-off fee payment in kind.

Once all that had been deducted, as well as the commis-
sions of various people, the final balance was quite something
to behold: I'd probably earned several tens of thousands of
euros, but the sum actually paid into my account was barely
10,000.

In September, instead of going to New York fashion week
where 'everyone was waiting for me', I went to the Sorbonne
to start a degree in philosophy. The following year I began
studying at the Cours Florent and the year after that I moved
to London to complete my degree in drama studies at
Roehampton University.

I came to life again.

I partied, I acted, I made love, I worked on various projects,
I made friends, I met a wonderful guy and I got my very first
job, at Shakespeare's Globe Theatre. And I became an adult,
more or less.

And now, after finally following Kate Staddon's advice and
studying at the London Academy of Music and Dramatic Art,
I'm more certain than ever that what I want to do is become

an actress. I'm going to devote all my time and energies to making this lifelong dream come true.

Granddaddy is no longer with us and I think about him all the time. I miss him terribly every day. I still feel afraid, sometimes terribly afraid, just like he did. I think he spent his whole life being afraid.

I'm not cold any more and my periods have returned. I'm a lot less irritable and my brain is working much better since I've been nourishing it with more than just knowledge and theatre and literature. I've learned to my cost that for it to function well, it needs protein, vitamins, omega-3s and iron. In short, everything that offers it a balanced diet, without which it gradually loses all its faculties. Which doesn't mean that my relationship with food is no longer difficult and complicated. I eat too much, or I don't eat at all and then I eat too much all over again. I still need time, I think, but that's not a problem.

I've got my whole life ahead of me.

Acknowledgements

Thank you to Alexis, my kindred spirit, who makes the world look more beautiful to me.

Thank you to Léopold for his seasoned reader's eye and his capacity to lend an ever kind and attentive ear.

Thank you to my angels, Naomi, Julia and Erwin. You are pure diamonds. I love you and you will always have a special place in my heart.

Thank you to the fairy Sabrina Philippe for helping me to rebuild my inner world.

Thank you to my lucky star Virginie Morgon who guides me through life in order to find my own way.

Thank you to my darling best friends, Romane and Alexandre, who support me and put up with me and know me inside out.

246

Thank you to my friends, on whom I rely so much and who contribute so much to my life: Paul, Lucille, Aliénor and Marie, Conlan, Guillaume, Sophie, Christian, Quentin, Larisa, Thomas and Marion.

Thank you to my uncle Gilles Dauxerre for his precious advice from a journalist's perspective.

Thank you to Debbie Seymour, Robert Price and Colin Hurley who, as well as being wonderful drama teachers, are also genuine life mentors.

Thank you to Jean-Baptiste Bourrat who is at the origin of this book. You have restored my faith in people, you have changed my way of thinking. You have helped me to grow. You have changed my life. You are my godfather and a member of my family from now and for ever. Thank you a thousand times for being who you are and for being in my life.

Finally, thank you to the exceptions whom I will never forget: Russell Marsh, Bouba, Phillip Lim, Stephan Janson, Daniel Peddle, Phoebe Philo, Samuel Drira, Vanessa Bruno, Olivier Rizzo, Damien Blottière, Francesca, Céleste and Louise.

Some names have been changed, however all events are based on real instances in the fashion industry.